Great American Writers

TWENTIETH CENTURY

EDITOR
R. BAIRD SHUMAN
University of Illinois

T. S. Eliot • Ralph Ellison

William Faulkner • Edna Ferber • F. Scott Fitzgerald

Horton Foote • Robert Frost

MARSHALL CAVENDISH
NEW YORK • TORONTO • LONDON • SYDNEY

Marshall Cavendish
99 White Plains Road
Tarrytown, New York 10591-9001

Website: www.marshallcavendish.com

© 2002 Marshall Cavendish Corporation

Salem Press

Editor: R. Baird Shuman
Managing Editor: R. Kent Rasmussen

Manuscript Editors: Heather Stratton
Lauren M. Mitchell
Assistant Editor: Andrea Miller
Research Supervisor: Jeffry Jensen
Acquisitions Editor: Mark Rehn

Marshall Cavendish

Project Editor: Marian Armstrong
Editorial Director: Paul Bernabeo

Designer: Patrice Sheridan

Photo Research: Candlepants
Carousel Research
Linda Sykes Picture Research
Anne Burns Images

Indexing: AEIOU

Library of Congress Cataloging-in-Publication Data

Great American writers: twentieth century / R. Baird Shuman, editor.
v. cm.
Includes bibliographical references and indexes.
Contents: v. 4. Agee-Bellow--v. 2. Benét-Cather--v. 3. Cormier-Dylan--v. 4. Eliot-Frost--v. 5. Gaines-Hinton--v. 6. Hughes-Lewis--v. 7. London-McNickle--v. 8. Miller-O'Connor--v. 9. O'Neill-Rich--v. 10. Salinger-Stein--v. 11. Steinbeck-Walker--v. 12. Welty-Zindel--v. 13. Index.
ISBN 0-7614-7240-1 (set)—ISBN 0-7614-7244-4 (v. 4)
1. American literature--20th century--Bio-bibliography--Dictionaries. 2. Authors, American--20th century--Biography--Dictionaries. 3. American literature--20th century--Dictionaries. I. Shuman, R. Baird (Robert Baird), 1929-

PS221.G74 2002
810.9'005'03
[B]
2001028461

Printed in Malaysia; bound in the United States

07 06 05 04 03 02   6 5 4 3 2 1

Contents

T. S. Eliot

BORN: September 26, 1888, St. Louis, Missouri
DIED: January 4, 1965, London, England
IDENTIFICATION: Modernist poet, dramatist, and critic, whose poetic style and complexity profoundly influenced the course of twentieth-century English poetry.

T. S. Eliot is celebrated as one of the premier poets of the twentieth century. His early work "The Love Song of J. Alfred Prufrock" startled the literary world in 1915 and was followed in 1922 by the most influential poem of the century, *The Waste Land*. His later poetry, exemplified by *Four Quartets* (1943), is marked by the essentially modernist notes of anxiety, the quest for individual identity in a depersonalized world, the function of words to express and/or conceal meaning, and the place of earthly and spiritual love in human life. Although he was American by birth, in 1927 Eliot became a British citizen and converted to the Church of England. His later works increasingly reflect religious themes and the struggle for spiritual renewal. He was awarded the Nobel Prize in literature for his poetry in 1948, and his works continue to be taught in schools and colleges.

The Writer's Life

On September 26, 1888, Thomas Stearns Eliot was born in St. Louis, Missouri, the son of Henry Ware Eliot, a businessman, and Charlotte Champe Stearns Eliot, a poet and biographer, both descendants of the settlers who came to seventeenth-century Massachusetts seeking religious freedom. The Eliots had settled in St. Louis after the poet's grandfather, the Reverend William Greenleaf Eliot, left New England in 1834 and founded the Unitarian Church of the Messiah as well as Eliot Seminary, which became Washington University under his leadership as chancellor in 1870. Eliot was raised in a family prominent in the commercial, civic, religious, and academic life of St. Louis.

Childhood. Eliot's early school days at Smith Academy in St. Louis and visits each summer to

This photograph of Eliot was taken in 1891, when he was three years old. Tom, as he was called then, was the youngest of seven children.

the picturesque seaside at Rockport and the fishing port of Gloucester, Massachusetts, made lasting impressions on him. In his later writing, he would include numerous references to the sea. One of his poems, part three of *The Four Quartets*, "The Dry Salvages," is named for Les Trois Sauvages, a small group of islands off the Gloucester coast. The nearby cities of Salem and Boston figured prominently in Massachusetts history as places where Eliot's forebears in the Massachusetts Bay Company helped to establish a theocracy. These places are present in much of Eliot's later writing, as the actual landscapes emerge in his imaginative, poetic landscapes.

With a writer mother and a university chancellor grandfather, Eliot had access to important sources of imaginative literature, including the Bible and a variety of poetry and prose, the classics among them. Heavily influenced by his mother and her love for the written word, Eliot grew up in an environment of writing and reading. His full-time return to Massachusetts to study at Milton Academy from 1904 to 1905 continued his exposure to literary classics and classical languages in preparation for his entry into Harvard University at age seventeen.

College. Eliot's years as a philosophy student at Harvard included the continued study of ancient languages and literatures, Pali and Sanskrit among them, and were marked by two principal influences on his thought. His exposure to the humanism of Irving Babbitt and the philosophy of George Santayana led Eliot to consider new areas of thought. His discovery of the French symbolist poets of the nineteenth century, first by reading Arthur Symons's *The Symbolist Movement in Literature* (1899) and then by reading the works of Jules Laforgue and other

Students at Milton Academy in Massachusetts sit at their desks in Wigglesworth Hall. When Eliot was sixteen, he studied classics at Milton Academy for one year before entering Harvard University. The date of this photograph is unknown.

French writers, set the stage for his own poetic experiments.

Upon completing his bachelor's degree in 1909, Eliot began work in Harvard's doctoral degree program. He completed his studies in 1914 and finished his doctoral dissertation on the philosophy of the British thinker F. H. Bradley in 1916, but he did not defend it. While a graduate student in 1910 and 1911, Eliot visited Germany and France and studied at the Sorbonne in Paris. The outbreak of World War I in 1914 made Eliot change his plans, from studying at Marburg, Germany, where he had received a fellowship, to moving to London and then to Merton College, Oxford University.

Important Encounters. In a meeting on September 22, 1914, that would alter the course of poetry in the twentieth century, Eliot introduced himself to the expatriate American

poet Ezra Pound. For the rest of his life Eliot would consult with Pound on his writing, allow Pound to edit much of his poetry, and revere his fellow poet as "the better craftsman"—a man to whom he dedicated *The Waste Land*. For his part, the iconoclastic Pound delighted in Eliot as a poet who rejected the outworn conventions of Victorian verse and wanted to breathe new life into poetry. Pound was startled upon reading Eliot's "The Love Song of J. Alfred Prufrock," composed in 1910–1911, and became Eliot's champion, arranging to have his work published and acknowledged as representing something quite new in poetry.

A second major event in Eliot's life occurred on June 26, 1915, when he married Vivien Haigh-Wood, beginning an unhappy marriage that lasted until Vivien's death in 1947, although they had separated officially in 1933. This marriage helps to account for some of the

In addition to the many medals, prizes, and awards Eliot was given in recognition of his work, he also received a number of honorary degrees. Here, in November 1949, at the University of London, Eliot accepts an honorary degree from the Earl of Athlone.

Relief from Eliot's unchallenging bank work came when the publishing firm of Faber and Gwynn hired him as an editor in 1925. His earlier work as a correspondent for *The Dial* and the *Revue Française* and his editorship of the new journal he founded, *The Criterion*, more than qualified him for this position. After a year as Clark Lecturer at Trinity College, Cambridge, Eliot converted to the Church of England and became a British citizen, completing his transformation. His religious conversion from the Puritan faith of his forefathers to the established church they had rebelled against marked a new and deeper encounter with the spiritual dimensions of human life. His conversion resulted in his religious poem *Ash Wednesday* (1930), his play *Murder in the Cathedral* (1935), and the series of poems that would become the masterpieces of his maturity, *Four Quartets*, composed over the period 1935 through 1942 and appearing together in 1943.

Maturity and Last Years. Continuing to work on his poetic craft, Eliot began to explore verse drama in the 1930s and, under the influence of William Butler Yeats, tried to reestablish the form theatrically. With such plays as *The Rock* (1934); his most popular success, *The Cocktail Party* (1949); and others, he established a verse drama with religious and spiritual overtones and themes that reflected his own concerns. He also dabbled in the whimsical, creating *Old Possum's Book of Practical Cats* (1939), upon which the popular Andrew Lloyd Webber musical *Cats* (1981) is based.

Eliot's work received special recognition in 1948, when King George VI awarded him the Order of Merit and he also received the Nobel Prize in Literature. He was to receive more awards, prizes, medals, and honorary degrees in similar recognition of his work. Ten years after the death of his first wife in 1947, Eliot married Valerie Fletcher and finally found the marital happiness that had previously eluded him. He spent his last years publishing his collected works and writing literary criticism. Eliot died in England in 1965, leaving behind a vast and valuable poetic legacy.

themes the young writer explored, including alienation and emptiness. With marriage came more financial responsibilities, and Eliot earned a living teaching in schools and serving as an extension lecturer at Oxford in the years from 1915 to 1917. He joined Lloyd's Bank as a clerk in March 1917, and worked there until 1925, with the exception of a three-month medical leave in 1921, which he spent in a Swiss sanatorium, where he completed his major early work, *The Waste Land*.

Turning Points. The publication of *The Waste Land* in 1922 marked a major change in Eliot's life. In the years immediately preceding its publication, he had written and published several poems that helped to assure his popularity as a new voice in poetry. This new long poem made Eliot the toast of the post–World War I literary world and reshaped the course of twentieth-century poetry, assuring him a lasting place in the history of English literature.

HIGHLIGHTS IN ELIOT'S LIFE

1888	Thomas Stearns Eliot is born on September 26 in St. Louis, Missouri.
1906–1909	Studies at Harvard University with George Santayana and Irving Babbitt.
1909	Undertakes graduate studies at Harvard; begins writing early poems, including "Portrait of a Lady" and "The Love Song of J. Alfred Prufrock."
1910–1911	Studies in Germany and France.
1914	Begins doctoral research; study in Germany ended by outbreak of World War I; relocates to London, then Oxford, England; meets Ezra Pound.
1915	Publishes first major poem, "The Love Song of J. Alfred Prufrock," in Chicago; marries Vivien Haigh-Wood; takes several jobs teaching in London, reviewing books, and editing *Egoist*, a literary magazine.
1917	Publishes first book of poetry, *Prufrock and Other Observations*; begins work at Lloyd's Bank, where he is employed for eight years.
1920	Publishes first book of literary criticism, *The Sacred Wood*.
1921	Becomes London correspondent for *The Dial*; spends three months in a Swiss sanatorium, finishing *The Waste Land*.
1922	Founds and edits *The Criterion*; becomes London correspondent for *Revue Française*; wins *Dial* award for *The Waste Land*.
1925	Joins firm of Faber and Gwynn; writes "The Hollow Men."
1926	Is appointed Clark Lecturer at Trinity College, Cambridge.
1927	Joins the Church of England; becomes British citizen.
1932	Is appointed Charles Eliot Norton Professor of Poetry at Harvard University.
1935	Produces early play *Murder in the Cathedral*.
1943	Publishes *Four Quartets*.
1947	Vivien Eliot dies.
1948	Eliot receives the Order of Merit from King George VI and the Nobel Prize in Literature.
1957	Marries Valerie Fletcher.
1958	Produces last play, *The Elder Statesman*.
1965	Dies in London on January 4; ashes interred in the parish church of East Coker, Somerset; memorial erected in Poet's Corner of Westminster Abbey, London.
1971	Valerie Eliot edits *The Waste Land: A Facsimile and Transcript of the Original Drafts Including the Annotations of Ezra Pound*.
1981	Andrew Lloyd Webber creates *Cats*, a musical based on Eliot's *Old Possum's Book of Practical Cats*.
1984	Michael Hastings writes *Tom and Viv*, a play about the Eliots' stormy marriage.
1988	Valerie Eliot edits *The Letters of T. S. Eliot: Volume I, 1898–1922*.
1994	Brian Gilbert directs the film version of *Tom and Viv*.
1996	Christopher Ricks edits Eliot's *Inventions of the March Hare: Poems, 1909–1917*.

The Writer's Work

Although T. S. Eliot wrote plays, literary criticism, and other nonfiction, he is known primarily by the title he most prized, that of poet. His most important poetry is characterized by a self-conscious, indirect place in poetic tradition, a sense of social alienation and of seeking after true identity, and a profound awareness of humanity's spiritual dimension, embodied in secular humanism in his early poetry and Christian humanism in his later works.

Issues in Eliot's Poetry. Among Eliot's many objectives as a poet was to "purify the language of the tribe," as he sometimes put it. He wanted to find a combination of words that would capture a mood, a feeling, a state of emotion, or a state of mind. He especially wanted to find in words an "objective correlative" between an idea and the phrase that could express that idea, a concept he explored in his essay "Hamlet" (1919).

Eliot also wanted to create an art that was impersonal, a poetry that would not express the writer's personality but would express an emotional state in which others could find resonances and meaning. This impersonality in art is a notion he elaborated on in his essay "Tradition and the Individual Talent" (1919). A third large poetic concern of Eliot's was a conscious use of traditions of poetry, drama, literature, and culture in his own verse. He strove throughout his works to belong to poetic traditions, while at the same time he changed the traditions in which he wrote, adding his own works and individual talent to the storehouse of tradition.

Eliot's Characters. A few of the characters that fill Eliot's works have become household words in his century. Madame Sosostris (famous clairvoyant), Mr. Eugenides, the Smyrna merchant, and Tiresias from *The Waste Land* are familiar characters to those who read Eliot in schools, as is the Sweeney of several of Eliot's works and J. Alfred Prufrock of Eliot's 1915 poem, "The Love Song of J. Alfred Prufrock."

His dramatic characters may be less memorable, except for the historical figure Thomas Becket, the subject of his play *Murder in the Cathedral*. Noteworthy in his own right, Eliot's

Edvard Munch's 1894 painting *Anxiety* (Munch Museet, Oslo, Norway) reflects Eliot's objectives in his poetry. While strongly expressing the anxious emotional state of the subjects depicted, the painting displays the impersonality Eliot sought in his poems.

The Subway (Whitney Museum of American Art, New York, New York), a 1950 painting by George Tooker exemplifies Eliot's poetic depiction of an alienated society, a society looking for its own identity.

Becket influenced a more widely known character created by the French playwright Jean Anouilh in his *Becket: Ou, l'Honneur de Dieu* (1959; *Becket: Or, The Honor of God*, 1960). By far the most popular of Eliot's characters are his "practical cats"—Growltiger, the Jellicles, Rum Tum Tugger, Mungojerrie, Rumpelteazer, Macavity, and Mr. Mistoffeles—and the other feline creatures who populate *Cats*, the popular Andrew Lloyd Webber work for musical theater adapted from Eliot's *Old Possum's Book of Practical Cats*.

Eliot's Literary Legacy. Some literary and cultural critics have referred to the twentieth century as the Age of Eliot. However, such a designation overstates Eliot's importance in the era; a reaction to his immense popularity at midcentury set in during the decades following his death. Nonetheless, Eliot's prominence in the history of poetry in English remains unquestionably high, although his work as an essayist and dramatist looms less important. It remains to be seen whether the modernism which he and Ezra Pound espoused and promulgated early in the twentieth century constitutes a new way of making art that will endure.

In an opposing point of view, some critics have asserted that Eliot's modernism represents a late flowering of nineteenth-century romanticism updated for his time and containing all the elements celebrating the individual, alienation, isolation, and the search for meaning. Indeed, a look back at the late-Victorian expressions against which Eliot was in revolt shows that the revolution was more linguistic than philosophical. Later studies examining the sources of Eliot's theories illustrate that several of his claims to novelty amount to new formulations of older ideas. What made Eliot's work so new in its day was the way he expressed the ideas that had filled the poetry of his predecessors, casting away artificial language and substituting direct personal expression. In any case, no student of twentieth-century literature can avoid coming to terms with Eliot and his work.

SOME INSPIRATIONS BEHIND ELIOT'S WORK

T. S. Eliot's work was inspired by the places in which he lived and studied, by his family, friends, and, especially, the writers he read and admired. Eliot's mother, a poet and biographer, exerted a lasting influence on him as a literate and literary person who lived by words. The places where Eliot he grew up, in Missouri and New England, inform his poetry with visual images of landscape, seascape, and river. Even more important to his work was his experience of living, working, and writing in England for the majority of his life: English places, customs, people, institutions, and traditions are present in the majority of Eliot's writings. His conversion to the Church of England and his becoming a British subject in 1927 point to his assimilation into English life. The church, in particular, held great attractions for him and informs his poetry of the late 1920s and after with examinations of the spiritual life, of the life and adventures of the soul, and of the themes of individual human salvation and the communion of souls.

Eliot's sources of poetic inspiration, apart from the work of his friend and fellow poet Ezra Pound, were many and varied. They include the poetic works of Dante Alighieri, John Donne, and the metaphysical poets of seventeenth-century England; the plays of William Shakespeare and his contemporaries in the Elizabethan and Jacobean theater; and the French symbolist poets of the nineteenth century. Eliot read widely and deeply in philosophy and history as well as literature, material that he used to fill his poetry with allusions that strengthen and highlight his poetic themes and concerns.

This oil-on-canvas painting, *Gloucester, 1899* (The Newark Museum, Newark, New Jersey), shows the fishing port of Gloucester, Massachusetts. As a youth Eliot made yearly summer visits to the seaside in Massachusetts. Viewing seascapes such as this helped to shape much of the imagery in Eliot's later writing.

BIBLIOGRAPHY

Ackroyd, Peter. *T. S. Eliot. A Life*. New York: Simon and Schuster, 1984.

Bush, Ronald. *T. S. Eliot: A Study in Character and Style*. New York: Oxford University Press, 1984.

Danson, J. L., et al., eds. *A Concordance to the Complete Poems and Plays of T. S. Eliot*. Ithaca, N.Y.: Cornell University Press, 1995.

Gordon, Lyndall. *Eliot's Early Years*. Oxford, England: Oxford University Press, 1977.

_____. *Eliot's New Life*. Oxford, England: Oxford University Press, 1988.

Harwood, John. *Eliot to Derrida: The Poverty of Interpretation*. New York: St. Martin's Press, 1995.

Kenner, Hugh. *The Invisible Poet: T. S. Eliot*. New York: McDowell and Obolensky, 1959.

Margolis, John D. *Eliot's Intellectual Development, 1922–1939*. Chicago: University of Chicago Press, 1972.

Moody, A. David, ed. *The Cambridge Companion to T. S. Eliot*. Cambridge, England: Cambridge University Press, 1994.

Stead, C. K. *The New Poetic: Yeats to Eliot*. Philadelphia: University of Pennsylvania Press, 1975.

_____. *Pound, Yeats, and Eliot and the Modernist Movement*. New Brunswick, N.J.: Rutgers University Press, 1985.

T. S. Eliot on Stage

T. S. Eliot was one of the foremost writers of dramatic poems and monologues in the early twentieth century, but he also wrote seven works for the stage, beginning with the unfinished *Sweeney Agonistes* in 1932 and concluding with *The Elder Statesman* in 1958. Eliot, always interested in drama and a prolific writer of dramatic criticism, became seriously engaged with the idea of writing in verse for the stage upon meeting E. Martin Browne, director of religious drama for the diocese of Chicester, in 1930. Browne later directed all of Eliot's plays except *Sweeney Agonistes*.

Dramatic Beginnings. Eliot's *Sweeney Agonistes* was never completed, but it enjoyed an avant-garde vogue in a production by the Group Theatre in 1934 and a limited run in London's West End in 1935. Like his first effort, *The Rock*, produced in 1934, features poetic, choric speech in pronounced metrical verse reminiscent of Greek drama. *The Rock* is more a pageant than a play since it relies on a strong narrative rather than upon significant staged events. Eliot's first true play, *Murder in the Cathedral*, produced in 1935, was written for the Canterbury Festival and concerns the martyrdom of Thomas Becket in the cathedral at Canterbury in 1170. After playing at Canterbury, *Murder in the Cathedral* moved to the Mercury Theatre in London, played in London's West End, was broadcast by the British Broadcasting Company, and was televised in 1936. The United States Federal Theatre Project sponsored a New York debut of *Murder in the Cathedral*, also in 1936.

As a playwright, Eliot was most interested in reviving poetic drama. His first three efforts sacrificed dramatic action to poetic statement. Of the three, his play of Thomas Becket contains significant dramatic action in addition to long poetic passages from the Chorus of the Women of Canterbury, Becket, the Four Tempters and the Four Knights who commit the murder and then offer their defenses for having done it. One dramatic device Eliot learned from seeing his play in production was to have the same actors who played the Tempters play the Knights, making the spiritual and temporal foes Becket faced look and sound similar to each other.

Still, the fledgling playwright had to create action that would compel an audience to listen to the verse. He experimented with modified blank verse in *The Family Reunion*, produced in 1939 in a year that saw the closing of many of London's theaters as a result of German bombing during World War II. Once again, in *The Family Reunion*, the narrative language overshadows the dramatic

This scene from Eliot's *Murder in the Cathedral* shows Thomas Becket, played by John Westbrook, being murdered by Henry II's henchmen in Canterbury Cathedral. The photograph is from the 1970 production of the play, which was actually staged in Canterbury Cathedral in England.

events, the action remains minimal, and the play's construction seems little different from a series of expositions strung together. Eliot later summed up his work on the play as giving most attention to the verse at the expense of plot and character.

Still preoccupied with the conventions of Greek drama, Eliot included the Eumenides—the Furies of Greek mythology—first as characters played by actors, then, in later productions, as gauzy, indistinct figures. The inclusion of supernatural characters in a realistic play on a realistic set posed difficulties for

One of the "practical cats" as interpreted for a theatrical production of *Cats,* a musical based on Eliot's *Old Possum's Book of Practical Cats.*

audiences and for the playwright who could see, after several productions, that he had to suggest and not embody the effect he wanted. He finally decided in 1951 that the Furies should be cut from the cast and treated as visible only to certain characters and not to the audience.

Dramatic Success. His apprenticeship as a playwright finally over, Eliot scored major dramatic and critical success with *The Cocktail Party*, which premiered in 1949 at the Edinburgh Festival, opened on New York's Broadway in 1950, where it won three Tony Awards, and later played in London's West End. Still as concerned as ever about the spiritual life, Eliot nonetheless made his supernatural trio as human as possible. The angelic Alex appears as a world traveler, Harcourt-Reilly as a well-intentioned physician, and Mrs. Julia Shuttlethwaite as a busybody. Yet these three, like the Fates of Greek myth suddenly becoming the agents of divine Providence, go about fixing lives and mending human errors. While much action remains described rather than staged, some truly dramatic things happen in the course of the play.

Eliot used his gifts for verse, comedy, dramatic irony, and dramatic revelations in his two remaining plays, *The Confidential Clerk*, performed in Edinburgh and London in 1953 and on Broadway in 1954, and *The Elder Statesman*, performed in Edinburgh and London in 1958 and making its American premiere in Milwaukee, Wisconsin, in 1963. Although not as popular or successful as *The Cocktail Party*, his last two plays do work in production. The comedy in each is restrained; the spiritual dimension of uncovering and confessing the past in preparation for the future is understated but focused; the conflicts in the plays are realistic and give rise to action on stage that is fundamental to any play.

In 1981 Eliot's poetry again reached the London stage in the popular musical *Cats*, which also opened on Broadway in 1982. Eliot won a posthumous Tony Award for the book, based on his *Old Possum's Book of Practical Cats* (1939), and, with Andrew Lloyd Webber, another for the musical score.

SOURCES FOR FURTHER STUDY

Eliot, Thomas Stearns. "Poetry and Drama." In *Selected Prose of T. S. Eliot*, edited by Frank Kermode. New York: Farrar, Straus and Giroux, 1975.

Malamud, Randy. *T. S. Eliot's Drama: A Research and Production Book*. Westport, Conn.: Greenwood Press, 1992.

Smith, Carol H. *Eliot's Dramatic Theory and Practice*. Princeton, N.J.: Princeton University Press, 1963.

JOHN J. CONLON

Reader's Guide to Major Works

FOUR QUARTETS

Genre: Poetry
Subgenre: Lyric verse
Published: London, 1943
Time period: 1930s and 1940s
Setting: Towns in England; islands off the coast of Massachusetts

Themes and Issues. Each of the *Four Quartets* explores spiritual transcendence over the physical and living a spiritual life. Although T. S. Eliot would continue to write verse for the remaining twenty-two years of his life, this poem is a masterpiece of his poetic maturity and the capstone of his career as a poet. In it he explores as fully as possible—in deceptively simple language—his spiritual heritage, questions, and dilemmas, his sense of history, and his experience of revelations of life's meaning. No longer out to startle the poetic world or to showcase his learning, Eliot strives in these poems to communicate directly, clearly, simply, and lyrically without the allusive trappings of his earlier verse.

The Poems. "Burnt Norton," the first of the poems, composed in 1935, was formed from lines Eliot had thought to use in his first completed play, *Murder in the Cathedral*, but which he excised from the working script. The title refers to a country house with a rose garden in the Cotswolds in England. The poem begins with two epigraphs from Heraclitus, the Greek philosopher of flux, which may be translated,

Theresa Stannard's painting *The Cottage Garden,* in its simplicity and lyrical beauty, reflects the tenor of Eliot's "Burnt Norton," the first poem in *Four Quartets.*

"While the Law of Reason [Logos] is common, the majority of people live as though they had an understanding of their own," and "The way upward and downward are one and the same."

These epigraphs are keys to understanding Eliot's message. In the first place, Heraclitus connects the divine attribute of eternity to the universal Logos (word), a term Eliot also associates with the Word of the Christian Gospel of Saint John. Heraclitus and Eliot consider a universe without a beginning, an eternal place where the individual soul participates in eternity. The sameness of the ways up and down represents a paradox Eliot explores consistently in the soul's journey. The poem's five parts, then, work together to present reflections on time and eternity, on the need for the individual to redeem time for an eternal benefit, and on love (the rose symbols) as the still force that contrasts with the motions of desire.

"East Coker" was composed in 1940 and is named for the place in Somerset, England,

POETRY

1917 Prufrock and Other Observations
1919 Poems
1920 Ara Vos Prec
1922 The Waste Land
1925 Poems, 1909–1925
1930 Ash Wednesday
1931 Triumphal March
1932 Sweeney Agonistes
1934 Words for Music
1936 Collected Poems, 1909–1935
1939 Old Possum's Book of Practical Cats
1943 Four Quartets
1954 The Cultivation of Christmas Trees
1962 The Complete Poems and Plays
1963 Collected Poems, 1909–1962
1967 Poems Written in Early Youth
1969 The Complete Poems and Plays
1971 The Waste Land: A Facsimile and Transcript of the Original Drafts Including the Annotations of Ezra Pound, ed. Valerie Eliot
1996 Inventions of the March Hare: Poems, 1909–1917

PLAYS

1932 Sweeney Agonistes (fragment)
1934 The Rock
1935 Murder in the Cathedral
1939 The Family Reunion
1949 The Cocktail Party
1953 The Confidential Clerk
1958 The Elder Statesman
1962 Collected Plays

NONFICTION

1917 Ezra Pound: His Metric and His Poetry
1920 The Sacred Wood
1924 Homage to John Dryden
1927 Shakespeare and the Stoicism of Seneca
1928 For Lancelot Andrewes
1929 Dante
1931 Thoughts After Lambeth
1931 Charles Whibley: A Memoir
1932 John Dryden: The Poet, the Dramatist, the Critic
1932 Selected Essays
1933 The Use of Poetry and the Use of Criticism
1934 After Strange Gods
1934 Elizabethan Essays
1936 Essays Ancient and Modern
1939 The Idea of a Christian Society

1942 The Music of Poetry
1942 The Classics and the Man of Letters
1948 Notes Toward the Definition of Culture
1950 Selected Essays
1951 Poetry and Drama
1953 The Three Voices of Poetry
1954 Religious Drama: Medieval and Modern
1955 The Literature of Politics
1956 The Frontiers of Criticism
1957 On Poetry and Poets
1964 Knowledge and Experience in the Philosophy of F. H. Bradley
1965 To Criticize the Critic
1988 The Letters of T. S. Eliot: Volume I, 1898–1922

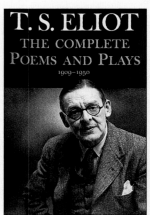

from which Eliot's ancestors emigrated in the seventeenth century and where Eliot himself would eventually be buried in 1965. In this poem, Eliot looks at family history as well as personal history and examines both in relation to the progress of the soul. He also considers the role of the poet, the craftsman of words, and the power and, at the same time, poverty of language to express adequately the concept of the divine.

The third of the quartets, "The Dry Salvages," was composed in 1941 and is named for a small group of islands off the Massachusetts coast near Gloucester, where Eliot spent his youthful summers. The poem also features Eliot's sense of personal geography, including his life along the Mississippi River. Probing the intersection of the timeless with time that he calls an occupation for the saint, Eliot alludes to God; to the Annunciation to Mary, Mother of God; and to Krishna. He also includes a prayer to the Queen of Heaven as he searches for artistic wholeness and spiritual health.

"Little Gidding," composed in 1942, is named for a place of spiritual refuge and activity in seventeenth-century England that represents a mystic place in Eliot's present. It is his most mature poetic statement of the nature of the spiritual life. It is Eliot's synthesis of the disparate elements that preoccupied him as a poet and includes near its end a highly charged, lyrical celebration of the poet's work as a unifying, health-giving activity. What Eliot seems to have discovered in the poetry of his maturity was the very thing that impelled him all his life: the power of the word to unify as well as to give, sympathize, and control.

Analysis. Structurally, the poems in this series follow the five-part sequence Eliot had used to great advantage in *The Waste Land*. These five parts, modeled on the movements of a quartet or a sonata, explore themes and variations on themes, always returning to the initial theme, or melody. The first part of each poem deals with the movement of time and the glimpses of eternity one has as time passes. The second part concerns worldly experience, which inevitably leads to a sense of dissatisfaction. The third part of each poem centers upon a need for purgation and the elimination of desires for earthly things. Part 4 of each poem is a lyric prayer of intercession or a recognition of the need for such intercession. The final section of each poem delves into the problem of achieving artistic wholeness, which becomes a metaphor for gaining spiritual health.

SOURCES FOR FURTHER STUDY

Asher, Kenneth G. *T. S. Eliot and Ideology*. Cambridge, England: Cambridge University Press, 1995.

Bodelsen, Carl A. *T. S. Eliot's "Four Quartets."* Copenhagen, Denmark: Copenhagen University Publications Fund, 1958.

Lobb, Edward, ed. *Words in Time: New Essays on Eliot's "Four Quartets."* London: Athlone, 1993.

Moody, A. D. *Thomas Stearns Eliot, Poet*. Cambridge, England: Cambridge University Press, 1979.

PRUFROCK AND OTHER OBSERVATIONS

Genre: Poetry
Subgenre: Dramatic monologue
Published: London, 1917
Time period: 1910s
Setting: Unspecified

Themes and Issues. Eliot announced the principal themes of his early literary life in this volume's title poem, "The Love Song of J. Alfred Prufrock" and provided variations on these themes in the other twelve poems in the collection. Chief among his themes are the question of identity, the search for it, the fear of rejection, the confusion that sometimes results from interpersonal relationships, and a sense of the absurdity of people and situations in which they find themselves.

The Poems. The range of deep issues with which Eliot concerns himself in such poems as "Portrait of a Lady," "Rhapsody on a Windy Night," and "La Figlia che Piange" jostle against more seemingly straightforward pieces in the collection, such as "Aunt Helen," "Cousin Nancy," and "The *Boston Evening Transcript*."

However, the poems in the volume are all of a piece, because they represent facets of Eliot's poetic delving into his own mysterious life and that of another human being, into a world both strikingly familiar and hauntingly unfamiliar. The title poem, then, sets the mood for the remainder of the book and influences readings of the other poems. Startlingly new in their own time, the poems puzzled and intrigued their first readers and have continued to puzzle and bewilder subsequent generations.

"The Love Song of J. Alfred Prufrock" is a dramatic monologue that is heavily influenced by the symbolist poets of late-nineteenth-century France. In it, Eliot presents a fragmented world described by someone with a divided or fragmented consciousness. The speaker seeks to have the listener (reader) take a journey with him, but the journey is perhaps more mental than it is physical.

The speaker worries about many things—about the possibility of an erotic encounter as well as the possibility that it will not take place, about his appearance, about what others think and say of him and that others will not think much or indeed anything of him. These preoccupations, along with some anxiety about his own image and worth, plague the speaker, who nonetheless feels that he is compelled to take the journey he invites the reader to share. Possibly because the problems that beset the speaker are so great and tangled, he does not arrive at any lasting conclusions about the encounter or about his own identity: He remains tentative, if negative, even at the end of the poem.

Depending on the angle at which it is seen, Diana Ong's painting *Conversion* presents different "faces" to the viewer, echoing the dichotomy and fragmentation of Prufrock's monologue in Eliot's *The Love Song of J. Alfred Prufrock.*

Analysis. Eliot provides several literary clues and allusions to what the self-consciously obscure and intricate title poem means. He first points to Dante Alighieri's character, Guido, from book 27 of the *Inferno* of *La divina commedia* (c. 1320; *The Divine Comedy*, 1802) in the poem's epigraph, thus setting the "Love Song" firmly in Hell. The reader, therefore, is listening to someone like Guido, who will speak without fear that what he says will be reported on Earth. The voice that addresses readers of the "Love Song" does so in scraps of phrases, parts of remembered conversations, and pieces of literary allusions. So, for example, the allusions to Michelangelo, to Saint John the Baptist, to Lazarus, to Hamlet and Polonius, and to mermaids lead the reader away from the "real" world into an imaginative world of myth, of literary invention, and of historical, dramatic, and biblical characters.

The voice quite possibly is also addressing itself in a dialogue between "self" and "soul" that reflects the division of self or the multiple personalities that the speaker seems to embody. The poem, then, like others in Eliot's first volume, seems to capture a dream or nightmare in words that suggest more than they state.

Such is also the case with "Preludes," "Rhapsody on a Windy Night," and other poems in the collection: They have the strangely eerie ring of nightmares spoken of in hushed voices. In "Portrait of a Lady," for example, Eliot has his speaker talk about friendships, which may appear to the reader to be hollow, as elements without which life would be a *cauchemar,* the French word for "nightmare." The odd metaphors in the poems suggest a high degree of nervousness, of self-consciousness, and, at times, of paralysis and inability to break out of the prisons of personality that each character seems to create. Eliot fills out his portrait gallery of eccentrics by adding the footman and the second housemaid from "Aunt Helen," the "new woman" in the person of "Cousin Nancy," and a strange assortment of characters, new and old, in "Mr. Apollinax."

SOURCES FOR FURTHER STUDY

Bergonzi, Bernard. *T. S. Eliot.* New York: Macmillan, 1962.

Sloane, Patricia. *Notes and Observations on T. S. Eliot's Early Poems.* November 15, 1999 (http://web. missouri. edu~tselist/sloaneO.htm).

Stead, C. K. *The New Poetic: Yeats to Eliot.* Philadelphia: University of Pennsylvania Press, 1975.

THE WASTE LAND

Genre: Poetry
Subgenre: Symbolist monologues
Published: New York, 1922
Time period: 1920s
Setting: Unspecified

Panel number 13, "Crops Left to Dry and Rot" (The Phillips Collection, Washington, D.C.), a painting from Jacob Lawrence's 1940–1941 series *The Migration of the Negro,* captures the barren emptiness suggested in the title of Eliot's long and most influential poem *The Waste Land.* This painting, showing one of the results of the Negro migration from the rural South, epitomizes many of the themes Eliot addresses in *The Waste Land.*

Themes and Issues. *The Waste Land* is one of the most influential and most discussed poems of the twentieth century. In it, Eliot continues his exploration of concerns he outlined and probed in his first volume of poetry and in a poem he considered to be a "prologue" to *The Waste Land*, "Gerontion" (1920). It is advisable, then, to approach this masterpiece of Eliot's poetic youth by first reading the poems he had already published. The themes of the poem—aridity, the burden of history, the function of memory, the issue of spirituality, the perplexing problems of sexuality and love, and the need to find meaning by shuffling personal, historical, and mythological experience—may make more sense if seen in relation to his earlier work. The issue of making sense out of life by examining others' experience remains central to Eliot's poetry. Likewise, dealing with the issue of the place of the individual in a host of cultural traditions is key to his writing.

The Poems. *The Waste Land* is actually a series of five poems linked together by the spiritual vision of the blind prophet from Greek drama, Tiresias, the poetic heir of Gerontion. Part 1, "The Burial of the Dead," floods the reader with images drawn from German, French, and English literature, the tarot pack, and other sources. The keynotes of the piece are the movement of time (day, season, year, centuries) and change from youth to age in a season of dreaded rebirth that begins the cycle anew each year. Part 2, "A Game of Chess," joins the mythic with the everyday, as does the first part, revealing dissatisfaction with the physical and sexual (Lil and Philomel) and disenchantment with the emptiness of luxury in which every move is ritualized, as in a chess game. The end of this section of the poem refers to a barman's call in an English pub and the Advent cry of the early Christian church, "HURRY UP PLEASE IT'S TIME."

The poem's third part, "The Fire Sermon," introduces Tiresias along with the Fisher King, Saint Augustine, and the Buddha as representative of the refining fire of the title. Set against them are the furtive encounters along the Thames, scenes in a canoe and in a flat, the tryst between Sweeney and Mrs. Porter, and Mr. Eugenides' unseemly proposition. These last sexually charged earthly encounters are purged by a meeting of Eastern and Western spirituality, which through fire frees the spirit from earthly bonds. Here, in the voice of Tiresias, Eliot's technique of uniting the whole poem into the seer's vision begins to work.

The brief (ten lines) fourth part, "Death by Water," recalls the opening of the poem and uses water, after fire, to effect another cleansing of the soul for a more spiritual life in a continuing paradox of death in life and life in death. Part 5, "What the Thunder Said," begins the process of refreshing the dry wasteland as the thunder speaks words from the Upanishads that may be translated as the keys to successful life: give, sympathize, control. Actual rain and spiritual wisdom thus bring about the rebirth of the land and those living in it as Eliot concludes his investigation of life among the ruins.

Analysis. In his notes to the poem, Eliot made much of the blind prophet Tiresias. He claimed that what the prophet sees is the substance of the work. He also stated that all the male characters merge into one and all the female characters blend into one, as the two sexes meet in the androgynous Tiresias. What Tiresias sees in his visionary or dreamlike state, then, becomes what the poet and the reader see or dream from their different vantage points in time. Furthermore, a key to understanding the poem as a symbolist piece comes in line 431, when Eliot's speaker claims that he has shored up the fragments of speech, action, thought, memory, and allusion against his ruins. These ruins of culture, history, and civilization fill the poem and inform the reader's response to it.

SOURCES FOR FURTHER STUDY

Bedient, Calvin. *He Do the Police in Different Voices: The Waste Land and Its Protagonist*. Chicago: University of Chicago Press, 1986.

Brooker, Jewel, and Joseph Bentley. *Reading the Waste Land: Modernism and the Limits of Interpretation*. Amherst: University of Massachusetts Press, 1990.

Eliot, Valerie, ed. *The Waste Land: A Facsimile and Transcript of the Original Drafts Including the Annotations of Ezra Pound.* New York: Harcourt Brace Jovanovich, 1971.

Gish, Nancy K. *The Waste Land: A Poem of Memory and Desire.* Boston: Twayne Publishers, 1988.

Hinchliffe, Arnold. *The Waste Land and Ash Wednesday.* Atlantic Highlands, N.J.: Humanities Press International, 1987.

Other Works

ASH WEDNESDAY (1930). This poem, like so many of T. S. Eliot's works after his conversion to Anglo-Catholicism, adds a specifically religious element to his usual accounts of struggles between the flesh and the spirit. Named for the traditional Christian day of mortification before fasting forty days (six weeks) before Easter, the poem contains six parts, one for each of the weeks, beginning in darkness and ending in light.

The poem opens with a hopeless statement, continues with a prayer for mercy and holy indifference, and moves to a refrain from the prayer Ave Maria. As in *The Waste Land*, Eliot's women in *Ash Wednesday* become one woman, as the Lady merges into the Mother of God, the Church, Theology, and the Blessed One.

The poem's second part reads like the prayer of a litany, while part 3 features a prayerful ascent past two specific temptations

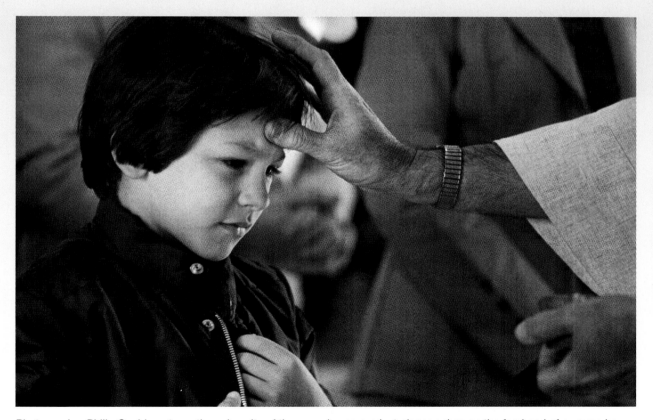

Photographer Philip Gould captures the solemnity of the occasion as a priest places ashes on the forehead of a young boy in Cocteau, Louisiana. Blessed ashes are given out to members of Catholic and Anglo-Catholic communities as a symbol of mortification on Ash Wednesday, the first day of the Lenten season of denial and fasting. Eliot's poem *Ash Wednesday* mirrors the spiritual Lenten passage from Ash Wednesday to Easter Sunday.

and into a spiritual realm. Part 4 heightens the spiritual journey, as the speaker asks for redemption of time and concludes with a phrase from another prayer to Mary, Mother of God, the Salve Regina. Part 5 looks forward to the spiritual and religious concerns that Eliot would bring to the writing of *Four Quartets* as he meditates on the power of the Word (Logos) and echoes various parts of the Anglican Mass and services for Holy Week. Clearly, the poet of anxiety and self-doubt had, by the time he composed this poem, become a poet of spiritual affirmation.

"THE HOLLOW MEN" (1925). This poem marks a major thematic turning point in Eliot's poetic practice. Always concerned with the spiritual aspect of man in his earlier poetry, Eliot added a specifically religious dimension to the end of this poem.

The poem opens with a citation from Joseph Conrad's novel *Heart of Darkness* (1902), announcing the death of the infamous Kurtz, and with another citation drawn from the children's petition on Guy Fawkes Day, celebrated in England on November 5, seeking donations for their stuffed effigies and bonfires. Eliot has a

The speakers who address the audience in Eliot's poem *The Hollow Men* are soulless straw figures, based on Guy Fawkes Day effigies. Fawkes, a conspirator in the Gunpowder Plot, was executed after the plot to blow up the English Parliament on November 5, 1604, was discovered just in time. This 1790 engraving, *The Fifth of November* by Charles Knight, shows children preparing to hang and set afire a stuffed Guy Fawkes effigy, a tradition still practiced in England today.

group of these effigies, hollow men, address the reader, telling their stories in this five-part poem.

Eliot's speakers talk, in part 1, of death's double kingdom, one in this world and in the next; of death's other kingdom, sleep (part 2); and a dead land (part 3) not unlike the Waste Land of his earlier poem. The poem's fourth part, also filled with negation, pictures a group of hollow men waiting by a river for the only release possible from their waiting, death. The only positive notes in the work come near the poem's end when a double chorus repeats words from the ending of the Anglican version of the Lord's Prayer, as if some small hope of spiritual consolation is finally possible to them in an otherwise empty, arid, and hollow existence. It is precisely this small glimmer of hope that may reflect Eliot's own turning toward the Church of England, which he completed with his conversion in 1927.

MURDER IN THE CATHEDRAL (1935). Eliot's first completed play in verse, this dramatization of the last days and martyrdom of Thomas Becket (1118–1170), Archbishop of Canterbury, was first presented at the Canterbury Festival in June of 1935 under the direction of E. Martin Browne. Eliot had long wanted to reestablish poetic drama as a viable theatrical form and had experimented with dramatic fragments in the years before he wrote the drama of Becket's murder.

The Chorus of the Women of Canterbury functions like the chorus in classical Greek tragedy, commenting on the action, foreshadowing events, and giving personal reflections on their meaning. Much of the play's interest lies in the interaction between Becket and the four tempters who offer him visions of good times, restoration of his temporal power as the king's chancellor, even greater power if he joins in a coup against the king and, finally, victory over King Henry through martyrdom. Here is precisely the dilemma that Eliot poses for Becket: Is it wrong or right to seek martyrdom? Does the end, proving oneself right and the king wrong, justify the means of seeking one's death? Do they who seek to lose their lives, in biblical phrase, save them?

The action of the second act, the martyrdom of Becket by four of the king's knights and the justification that the murderers give for themselves also pose moral questions that Eliot would have his audience confront. The Christmas sermon between acts 1 and 2 provides a key to the entire play as a sermon drawn from the life of a saint, a parable for the modern world concerning actions and their motives.

"TRADITION AND THE INDIVIDUAL TALENT" (1919). This early essay of Eliot's quickly became what he called his most influential prose work. It established him as a critic who set a new tone in the writing of aesthetic theory. While it typified Eliot's early critical stance, it also reflected his poetic practice. Because, he posits, a poet's work belongs in a tradition, it becomes important for the critic to know what a poet shares with the dead poets, his ancestors. This discussion could easily be about his own early poetry, especially the allusive "The Love Song of J. Alfred Prufrock," which borrows liberally from classical and Renaissance writers. In his critical and poetic view, there is an ideal order of art that is complete before any poet writes. Once a poet adds to that order, modifying the work of previous poets, the order itself changes.

Eliot also focused in this essay on the impersonality of the poet, divorcing the personality of the writer from the work he produces. In an argument advanced by the French novelist Gustave Flaubert and the English critic Walter Pater, Eliot turns to science and compares the poet's mind to a piece of platinum introduced into a chamber filled with oxygen and sulphur dioxide. A chemical reaction takes place, but the platinum filament, the catalyst, remains unchanged. The poet, he asserts, is like that impersonal bit of platinum. This theory allowed Eliot the man to distance himself from the bizarre elements in the works of Eliot the poet.

Resources

T. S. Eliot's early critical position that poetry was an escape from personality may account for the dearth of material about this very private individual. Some of his correspondence has been collected and published by Valerie (Fletcher) Eliot, who otherwise steadfastly refused permission to quote from it. Moreover, about two thousand letters exchanged between Eliot and Emily Hale, a lifelong friend, remain sealed until the year 2020. Eliot resources, pages, and sites on the Internet are numerous, with most containing links to others. Some reliable Web resources include the following:

The Bartleby Archive at Columbia University. This Web site contains many of Eliot's early works legally available on the Web. (http://www.bartleby.com)

What the Thunder Said: Resources on T. S. Eliot. This Web site contains a time line, listing of works, other resources, an e-mail feedback option and links to other sites. (http://www.deathclock.com/thunder)

TSE: The Web Site. This is the official home page of the T. S. Eliot listserv, an on-line discussion group for scholars, students, and readers of Eliot's works. It is maintained by the University of Missouri and includes a concordance to Eliot's *Collected Poems* and links to other sites. (http://web.missouri.edu/~tselist.)

Academy of American Poets, Poetry Exhibits, T. S. Eliot. The Academy of American Poets has an informative Web site with a selected bibliography of Eliot's work, poems, and links to other Eliot sites. (http://www.poets.org/poets/poets.cfm?prmlD=18)

Voices & Visions: T. S. Eliot. A video series on the lives and works of thirteen modern American poets by Annenberg/CPB Multimedia features a program on T. S. Eliot. The company's Web site gives Eliot information and links to other relevant sites and also features a video clip of "The Love Song of J. Alfred Prufrock." (http://www.learner.org/catalog/literature/vvseries/vvspot/Eliot.html)

JOHN J. CONLON

Ralph Ellison

BORN: March 1, 1914, Oklahoma City, Oklahoma
DIED: April 16, 1994, Harlem, New York
IDENTIFICATION: Mid-twentieth-century African American novelist, scholar, and essayist best known for his penetrating examination of the position of the African American in modern U.S. society.

Ralph Ellison's perceptions about the "invisibility" of the African American citizen in modern U.S. life are described in his seminal work *Invisible Man* (1952), a novel that received both immediate acclaim and enduring fame. This novel has been termed one of the most important works of twentieth-century fiction. It has been read by millions and has influenced numerous younger writers. With *Invisible Man*, Ellison broke out of the mold of the black "protest" writer, presenting a stirring and haunting tale of one man's attempt to find his place in a racially and socially defined United States. Ellison became a powerful voice in American literature, and *Invisible Man* is widely taught in high school and college literature courses.

The Writer's Life

Ralph Waldo Ellison—named after the nineteenth-century essayist Ralph Waldo Emerson—was born on March 1, 1914, in Oklahoma City, Oklahoma. His father, Lewis Ellison, was an ice and coal vendor who died accidentally when Ellison was three years old. Ellison and his younger brother Herbert were then raised by their mother, Ida Milsap Ellison, who worked as a nursemaid, janitor, and domestic. She was influential in Ellison's life, and in her activities for Socialist Party politics and against segregation laws, she modeled a political awareness for her son. In addition to his mother, Ellison had numerous other role models: He attended a grammar school named for the legendary black leader Frederick Douglass and won a scholarship to Booker T. Washington's Tuskegee Institute.

Ellison's Childhood. Ellison was drawn to music at an early age. He began playing the trumpet at age eight and played in his high school band. His early interest in music led to his studying classical composition at Tuskegee Institute and greatly influenced his intellectual perspective later in life. Music—jazz, rhythm and blues, Negro spirituals—would play a large part in his famous novel *Invisible Man* and may even account for its balanced sentence structure and cadenced, rhythmic prose. In his adolescent years, Ellison worked in a drugstore patronized by local jazz musicians who exposed him to the latest trends. Additionally, his mother's African Methodist Episcopalian church familiarized him with spirituals and religious hymns. He dreamed of becoming a composer and having a career in music.

Ellison was also drawn to writing at a young age, and he later would note that his early exposure to the novels of Ernest Hemingway and the poetry of T. S. Eliot had somehow enabled him to get in touch with his own feelings about the black communities in which he had lived as a boy. Ellison remarked upon his debt to the Russian novelist Fyodor Dostoyevski's Underground Man, saying that it is no coincidence that his hero in *Invisible Man* lives in a "hole" and literally goes underground during the riot episode in Harlem.

Ellison's mother created an intellectually stimulating environment

Students of Tuskeegee Institute exit one of the older buildings on the Alabama campus in April of 1940. Ellison studied classical musical composition at the school on a scholarship from 1933 to 1936.

for her sons, bringing home books, magazines, and recordings in order to expose the boys to fascinating topics. She also filled their home with a variety of guests, both black and white. Ellison, unlike many of his contemporaries from the South, did not live a segregated life; his parents had many white friends who came to his house when he was small. Later he was to state that "any feelings of distrust I was to develop towards whites were modified by those with whom I had warm relations."

College Years.

In 1933 Ellison received a scholarship to study classical musical composition at the prestigious all-black Tuskegee Institute in Alabama. A testament to his tenacity is the fact that he traveled there by riding freight trains. However, Ellison felt alienated by off-campus racial segregation, something he had not experienced in the more liberal climate of Oklahoma City. He remained at his studies from 1933 until 1936, when, because of difficulties with his scholarship, he moved to New York City to earn money. There, he experienced the cultural life of Harlem's famous community of black artists and intellectuals.

The Fledgling Writer.

The Harlem that Ellison visited in the 1930s was not the city of the 1920s Harlem Renaissance. Its vitality had been lessened somewhat by the Great Depression, but it still held interest for his budding creative intellect. In Harlem, Ellison met many artists and writers, including the novelist Richard Wright and the poet Langston Hughes. He was also introduced to the politically charged works of the French writer André Malraux, whom he later claimed as an influence on his own work. The most dramatic event of this period was Ellison's conscious de-

This street scene in Harlem, looking east from Eighth Avenue on 125th Street (year unknown), reveals the rich cultural life that, although tempered by the Great Depression, was still an inspiration to Ellison in the late 1930s. The renowned Apollo Theater is on the left.

cision to give up music and his plans to return to Tuskegee. Under the tutelage of his new friend and mentor, Richard Wright, he instead devoted himself to writing.

In 1938 Ellison worked with the Federal Writers' Project, a division of the Works Progress Administration (WPA), a depression-era program designed to lower unemployment. Then in 1939 he began to publish short stories. As a result, he was asked to be managing editor of a new radical magazine called *Negro Quarterly*. In 1943 he joined the Merchant Marine, working as ship's cook and baker, while he continued to write stories. In the following year he published "King of the Bingo Game" and "Flying Home."

Married Life and *Invisible Man*. In 1946 Ellison married Fanny McConnell, a graduate of Fisk University who took a strong interest in his writing. They lived in a variety of places, in-

cluding Massachusetts, Rome, and different parts of New York. It was at this time that Ellison found himself hearing a voice that kept insisting, "I am an invisible man." This became the opening line of the novel that would make Ellison famous. Parts of the novel were published in literary magazines before its final publication in 1952. Ellison remained married to Fanny for forty-eight years, until his death in 1994. After his death, Fanny became the executor of his literary works, including the posthumously published *Juneteenth* (1999).

Invisible Man radically changed Ellison's life and brought him instant fame. In 1955 he received a fellowship from the American Academy of Arts and Letters to write a second novel, which was never published as a longer work, but appeared instead as various short stories. He also taught creative writing at New York University and served as a visiting scholar at many other institutions in the 1960s.

Ellison (far left) poses with five of the other six honorary degree recipients at Harvard University in Cambridge, Massachusetts, on June 13, 1974, prior to the commencement ceremony in which Ellison became a Doctor of Letters.

HIGHLIGHTS IN ELLISON'S LIFE

1914	Ralph Waldo Ellison is born on March 1 in Oklahoma City, Oklahoma.
1917	Loses father in accidental death.
1922	Begins trumpet lessons.
1933	Studies classical musical composition at Tuskegee Institute.
1936	Leaves Tuskegee and moves to New York City.
1937	Begins friendship with novelist Richard Wright.
1938	Works for Federal Writers' Project.
1939	Publishes first short stories and is asked to edit *Negro Quarterly*.
1943–1945	Serves in Merchant Marine.
1946	Marries Fanny McConnell.
1952	Publishes *Invisible Man*.
1953	Awarded the National Book Award for *Invisible Man*.
1955	Receives fellowship from American Academy of Arts and Letters to write second novel.
1964	Publishes essay collection *Shadow and Act*.
1974	Receives an honorary degree from Harvard University
1975	Attends dedication of Ralph Ellison Branch Library in Oklahoma City.
1986	Publishes *Going to the Territory*.
1994	Dies in Harlem, New York, of pancreatic cancer on April 16.
1999	His second novel, *Juneteenth*, is published posthumously.

Social and Political Context of Ellison's Work. During the late 1930s and early 1940s, many progressive blacks were joining the Communist Party in hopes of furthering their civil rights. Ellison, who had belonged to the racially mixed Merchant Marine, refused to join the Communist Party because it would not protest segregated military units. The 1960s were turbulent years for the Civil Rights movement, and many militant black leaders at-tempted to separate themselves from Ellison because he vehemently refused to join the movement for a separate black culture.

The Author's Later Life and Publications. During the 1960s, Ellison and Fanny purchased an old farm in Plainsfield, Massachusetts, where Ellison continued to work on his second, much-awaited novel. In 1964 he published *Shadow and Act*, a collection of essays.

As evidenced by Ellison's studies, music was a great inspiration for him. *Invisible Man* begins with an interior monologue in which the narrator talks to himself in his mind while listening to jazz. One critic has written an extended article claiming that the author uses the blues as a metaphor for African American history. Music, for Ellison, was a way to expand himself into a larger world, and it plays a large role in all of his works.

Ellison also acknowledges his debt to many writers, such as the Russian novelist Fyodor Dostoyevski and the American writer Ernest Hemingway. He was an accomplished scholar, and *Invisible Man* makes allusions, or references, throughout its pages to a number of authors and literary works. Ellison names characters in the novel after famous literary personalities and makes many references, puns, and quotes to literary works and historical events.

Finally, Ellison was motivated both by his mother, who inspired his intellectual inquiries and to whom he dedicated *Invisible Man*, and by his mentors, such as

Gil Mayers's painting *Swing* resonates with Ellison's passionate love of music. Music, Ellison's first love, is referenced throughout his works.

Wright and Hughes. These men helped ground Ellison's own liberal Oklahoma experiences and broaden his awareness by sharing their experiences of racial clashes in a segregated South.

Unfortunately, a fire at the farm in 1967 destroyed most of the revisions on the new novel. In 1970 Ellison received a literary award from the French government and continued lecturing at major universities. *Invisible Man* remained in print during all these years, as popular as ever, despite changing social times. In 1975 Ellison appeared at the dedication of the Ralph Ellison Branch Library in Oklahoma City. He received many honorary degrees and served on arts councils that fostered opportunities for new black writers and artists. In 1986 he published another collection of essays, *Going to the Territory*. Although he continued to maintain that he was completing his second novel, it was not forthcoming. In 1994, at the age of eighty, Ralph Ellison died of pancreatic cancer with his final work still unfinished.

The Writer's Work

While Ralph Ellison also wrote short stories and essays, he is best known for his major opus and groundbreaking novel, *Invisible Man*, and for his long-awaited second novel, *Juneteenth*, published after his death. His essays are collected in *Shadow and Act*, and various short stories are gathered in *Flying Home and Other Stories* (1996). It is *Invisible Man*, however, that has won Ellison a prominent place in American literature and has marked his writing as unique among African American authors. Its richly complex and lushly symbolic style skillfully captures various African American dialects. In its obituary on Ellison, *Time* magazine described *Invisible Man* as "gorgeously written, a phantasmagoric satire of mid-century life in Harlem and the American South."

Issues in Ellison's Fiction. Ralph Ellison once insisted that "Whatever else the true American is, he is also somehow black." Ellison implies that to truly know and understand the United States, one must understand the African American experience. This is a dominant issue in *Invisible Man*. The central issue, however, is not only the difficulty of being black, as shown throughout the unnamed hero's adventures, but also the experience of being black and essentially without identity, or "invisible," in a world where "others refuse to see me."

Ellison strove in *Invisible Man* to avoid the black protest novel popular with his contemporaries. Instead he attempted to create a more universal work that would establish him not only as an African American writer but also as

Like the literary works of Ellison, artist Robert Gwathmey's work focuses on both blacks and whites, their faces often obscured. His 1943 oil painting *Hoeing* invites the viewer to focus on the black individual in the forefront. The image echoes Ellison's belief that one must understand the African American experience to truly know and understand the United States.

a writer in a broader sense. Ellison did not seem to have an agenda to convince people how to deal with racism politically. Rather, he wanted to convey the personal experience of being "invisible" in the United States, where the black citizen is basically "unseen."

Ellison focused on communicating this complex sense of being invisible, believing that it was a detriment to both blacks and whites. This was a revolutionary idea for its time. Many other racial issues are involved in the novel, but *Invisible Man* specifically focuses on this characteristic in African American lives. The novel asks readers to consider how one should perceive, create, and give meaning to one's personal and social identity. It is a universal question with which literature continually wrestles.

People in Ellison's Fiction. Ellison peoples *Invisible Man* with a wide variety of characters who also operate on a symbolic level. They are individual and well-defined characters, but they are also representative of certain types or attitudes regarding the place of the African American in U.S. society. His most memorable characters tend to represent extremes of various ideas. Bledsoe, the "manager" of the black university that the narrator attends, is the long-suffering black man who has managed to grab some power for himself by telling the white college trustees what they want to hear. Todd Clifton is the African "prince" who cannot find a place of dignity in a society that forces him to be either a liar or an outcast. Brother Tarp represents the heritage of the slave days. Ras the Destroyer is a militant Black Panther type who seeks a return of all black citizens to their native Africa.

Ellison's white characters are equally fascinating, and often appear to be misguided or deluded in their attempts to advance the black cause. Mr. Norton, the college trustee, is clearly fooling himself about his role in the narrator's "fate," and Brother Jack, head of the Brotherhood, pretends to aid the black race while merely manipulating its members. Likewise, Senator Adam Sunraider in *Juneteenth* tries to deny the healing truth about his past life among blacks, instead promoting his clearly racist ideas.

Ellison creates characters who are a blend of unique personality and symbolic meaning. His characters, distinct and interesting, come from all walks of life—Jim Trueblood is a tenant farmer; Brother Jack is obviously highly educated—and infuse his works with a linguistic richness reflecting the diversity of American culture and language.

The Quest for Racial Identity. Ellison's use of characters emphasizes the problems faced by the unnamed narrator of *Invisible Man*. Although the many characters offer him diverse roles or ways of being, they do not present him with a satisfactory identity. What the narrator discovers and accepts is that a true sense of racial identity for the African American may be impossible. The quest for true identity cannot be satisfied by choosing to become a stereotype or what others expect him to be. Instead the "invisible man" must accept his invisibility and begin from that point to define himself by his

LONG FICTION

1952 Invisible Man
1999 Juneteenth

NONFICTION

1964 The Writer's Experience
1964 Shadow and Act
1986 Going to the Territory

SHORT FICTION

1944 King of the Bingo Game and Flying Home
1996 Flying Home and Other Stories

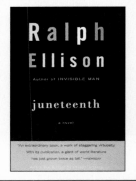

Jacob Lawrence's 1941 image *The Migration Gained in Momentum* (Museum of Modern Art, New York), part of Lawrence's *The Migration Series*, reflects the lack of identity experienced by the narrator in Ellison's 1952 novel, *The Invisible Man*, and the search to find it.

1955 to 1957 while on a fellowship from the American Academy of Arts and Letters. Excerpts were published in various literary magazines from 1959 to 1965, and Ellison had intended to deliver the manuscript to his publisher in late 1967. However, that autumn his home caught fire and most of the manuscript, which he was revising at the time, was destroyed. Despite this terrible blow, Ellison worked on rewriting the new novel and spoke of it as late as 1980. By the time of its posthumous publication in 1999, *Juneteenth* was mammoth in size. Ellison had envisioned it as a sprawling three-volume work, of which *Juneteenth* covers only the central events.

Although interest in *Juneteenth* has been high, a critical consensus of its contribution to American letters has not yet been made. Despite the controversy over whether *Invisible Man* is "a work particularly for blacks or a novel with universal import," the fact remains that it has greatly impacted how both whites and blacks think about what it means to be American.

moral choices. In a similar manner, *Juneteenth* deals with the quest for identity; in that novel it is presumably a white man who deals with the need to accept the meaning of his past, which is inextricably tied up with a black heritage.

Ellison's Critical Reception and Legacy.

Ellison's first novel was almost universally acclaimed by critics, who acknowledged its relevance to American thought and literature. In a 1965 poll of more than two hundred writers, critics, and editors, *Book Week* magazine named *Invisible Man* first in a list of the most memorable and enduring books. A critic in that poll called it "a veritable *Moby Dick* of the racial crisis." Many people eagerly awaited Ellison's next long work of fiction, but it did not appear until 1999.

Ellison stated that the idea for his second novel originated in 1951, even before he had completed *Invisible Man*. He worked on it from

BIBLIOGRAPHY

Bishop, Jack. *Ralph Ellison*. New York: Chelsea House, 1988.

Bloom, Harold, ed. *Major Modern Black American Writers*. Philadelphia: Chelsea House, 1995.

———. *Ralph Ellison: Modern Critical Reviews*. New York: Chelsea House, 1986.

Covo, Jacqueline. *The Blinking Eye: Ralph Waldo Ellison and His American, French, and Italian Critics*. Metuchen, N.J.: Scarecrow, 1974.

Eichelberger, Julia. *Prophets of Recognition: Ideology and the Individual in Novels by Ralph Ellison, Toni Morrison, Saul Bellow, and Eudora Welty*. Baton Rouge: Louisiana State University Press, 1999.

Mangione, Jerre. *The Dream and the Deal: The Federal Writers' Project, 1935–1943*. Boston: Little, Brown, 1972.

Nadel, Alan. *Invisible Criticism: Ralph Ellison and the American Canon*. Iowa City: University of Iowa Press, 1988.

Rosenblatt, Roger. *Black Fiction*. Cambridge, Mass.: Harvard University Press, 1974.

Schor, Edith. *Visible Ellison: A Study of Ralph Ellison's Fiction*. Westport, Conn.: Greenwood Press, 1993.

Whitlow, Roger. *Black American Literature: A Critical History*. Totowa, N.J.: Rowman and Allanheld, 1974.

Reader's Guide to Major Works

INVISIBLE MAN

Genre: Novel
Subgenre: Picaresque novel; social criticism
Published: New York, 1952
Time period: 1930s and 1940s
Setting: Unnamed southern state; Harlem, New York

Themes and Issues. The opening line of Ellison's masterpiece still reverberates a half-century after its publication: "I am an invisible man." Proclaimed one of "the great American novels," *Invisible Man* chronicles the journey of an unnamed protagonist/narrator through several adventures as he experiences life as a black man in a society dominated by white institutions. The narrator is a kind of black Everyman who must find a way to exist in a society that refuses to see him. He is at once a disembodied voice and a universal person on a voyage of self-discovery. Ellison succeeds in conveying the experience of being "invisible"—without solid, clear, or coherent identity in an America that refuses to see its black citizens clearly.

A deeper, more complex theme deals with all U.S. citizens—people of all races, religions,

Artist Romare Bearden, echoing the sentiments of Ellison's novel *Invisible Man*, said "I felt that the Negro was becoming too much of an abstraction . . . . What I've attempted to do is establish a world through art in which the validity of my Negro experience could live and make its logic." Like Ellison's novel, Bearden's collage *Mysteries*, one of a series of photomontages created by Bearden in 1964, seeks to highlight the importance of the African American experience.

cultures, and defining characteristics. The novel explores the damaging effects of an unbalanced power structure both to individuals and to society as a whole. Such a structure, which is slowly and painfully uncovered by the narrator as his consciousness expands, demands from its black citizens either a lack of identity or a false one.

Throughout the novel, the narrator proceeds from one adventure to another, finding that his choices for an identity are all either demeaning or distasteful to him. On the one hand his grandfather and Bledsoe offer him the example of playing along with white society and "yessing them to death." On the other hand, the Brotherhood demands total sacrifice of his individual identity for the betterment of the group (here, presumably the Communist Party). As the narrator comes to understand the role he must play or place he must take as a black man in the United States, he increasingly withdraws, finally ending up in his "warm hole." There he decides to "hibernate" and find out how best to become a real person, with real choices and an authentic identity.

What the narrator confronts on his way to self-realization and self-identity is that an identity based on the opinions or expectations of others is no identity at all. On a deeper level, Ellison suggests that if a white social system based its identity on not seeing its black citizens clearly and forced them into positions of inferiority, then the white members of such a society would also have no identity, because the whites' perceptions about their identities would be based on false premises about the weakness of others. Power based on weakness is not power at all. This complex and insightful assumption perhaps in part explains the chilling concluding line of the novel, "Who knows but that, on the lower frequencies, I speak for you?" The narrator is clearly asking each individual in his audience to consider the basis of his or her own identity.

The Plot. The novel begins at the end of the story and sets up the rest of the tale to be told as a flashback. By the end of the novel, the narrator has returned to the beginning of his story and its setting. The reader has been taken through a metaphoric voyage of discovery, experiencing both the struggle of the black man in America and the struggle within the mind of the narrator. The reader processes all of the novel's events and epiphanies along with the narrator. Therefore, the reader experientially knows what the first-person narrator knows.

The narrator begins his tale with a chapter called "Battle Royal," in which he has been invited to receive a scholarship and present a speech before a group of white town officials, "good old boys" who have been drinking. Before he is to receive the scholarship, the narrator must perform several humiliating and degrading acts, which include witnessing a striptease, fighting other black boys while blindfolded, and scrambling for money on an electrified carpet.

This chapter sets up several metaphors and symbols for the rest of the novel. They echo as repetitive lessons for the narrator, who must "learn" what he is not and does not want to be. In being forced to fight with other black boys, the narrator is faced with the choice either of cheating and peeking from under the blindfold or of making a deal and bribing another fighter to take a fall. The staged fight pits the boys against one another, metaphorically allowing the white men to exploit the boys' power and strength for their own destructive purposes.

The narrator is then allowed to give his speech, while swallowing back blood from his boxing match. He receives his scholarship, and his adventures continue through college, from which he is expelled for making an honest mistake. He migrates to New York City and takes his first job at Liberty Paints. There he makes a crucial mistake that results in an explosion. The narrator then finds himself in a very strange hospital where he undergoes a kind of identity loss and loses all idea of who he is. He endures numerous disastrous events and encounters several prophetic characters who attempt to clue him in to "the way things work." He then finds himself delivering a speech in support of a black family that is being evicted. His natural talent as a speaker is quickly noticed by a member of the Brotherhood. The narrator, still seeking to discover who he is, believes he has found meaning, destiny, and identity as a member of this "brotherly" organization.

After the narrator is betrayed by the Brotherhood, he has several encounters with white women and is almost murdered by the militant Ras the Destroyer in Harlem. He then escapes through a manhole and finds his way back to his "hole": a hidden basement where he has tapped into free power and heat. He has wired his ceiling with over thirteen hundred lights, and here he finally feels that he can be seen, at least figuratively. He proceeds to accept his invisibility and, even as an "invisible" man, to accept social responsibility.

Analysis. *Invisible Man* received the National Book Award upon its publication in 1952, and it has since been the focus of much literary and critical discussion. On one level, the novel can be seen as an indictment of U.S. racial policies and an illustration of the psychological legacy of political domination. On another level, it can be viewed as an optimistic call for a new interpretation of the search for African American identity. Ellison's narrator has a variety of choices for his position in American society: yes-man, social activist, African nationalist, deceptive saboteur, or social chameleon. Yet he settles for none of these dead ends; he will not accept the stereotypes or self-sacrificing roles that society offers to him. Instead he chooses and embraces invisibility as his identity in the belief that there is power in self-awareness. He believes that being invisible is not the worst thing in the world but that a lack of self-awareness is.

Ellison offers a new interpretation of the African American identity. It is an identity that is not based on anyone else's expectations. It is an identity that does not seek to tear down the existing society. It is an identity that functions as a social conscience. His hero states in the final paragraphs of the book, "I'm coming out, no less invisible . . . since there's a possibility that even an invisible man has a socially responsible role to play."

If the narrator does indeed "speak for us," as the final line of his tale suggests, then his powerful experiences illustrate the socially responsible role that he—and, Ellison suggests, all African Americans—must play, or there will eventually be no society left. African Americans must be authentic, productive, and responsible for their moral choices. In such a role, the Invisible Man suggests, his invisibility may end and he may truly be seen.

SOURCES FOR FURTHER STUDY

Hersey, John, ed. *Ralph Ellison: A Collection of Critical Essays.* Englewood Cliffs, N.J.: Prentice-Hall, 1974.

Marowski, Daniel G., ed. "Ralph Ellison." In *Contemporary Literary Criticism.* Vol. 54. New York: Gale Research, 1989.

O'Meally, Robert. *New Essays on "Invisible Man."* New York: Cambridge University Press, 1988.

Reilly, John M., ed. *Twentieth Century Interpretations of "Invisible Man."* Englewood Cliffs, N.J.: Prentice-Hall, 1970.

Schor, Edith. *Visible Ellison: A Study of Ralph Ellison's Fiction.* Westport, Conn.: Greenwood Press, 1993.

Trimmer, Joseph, ed. *A Casebook on Ralph Ellison's "Invisible Man."* New York: Thomas Y. Crowell, 1972.

JUNETEENTH

Genre: Novel
Subgenre: Social criticism
Published: New York, 1999
Time period: 1950s
Setting: Washington, D.C.

Themes and Issues. Ellison's editor and friend John F. Callahan described *Juneteenth* as "a mythic saga of race and identity, language and kinship, in the American experience." Like Ellison's first novel, *Juneteenth* draws from many African American methods of communication and expression, such as sermons, folktales, the blues, and jazz. The influences of Mark Twain and William Faulkner on the novel's style and content are evident. As in *Invisible Man,* this novel provides a rich cornucopia of language, full of imagery and meaning. The title refers to the date June 19, 1865, when Union troops landed in Galveston, Texas.

Michael Escoffery's 1996 painting *June Teenth* depicts a contemporary perspective of the arrival of Union troops in Galveston, Texas, on June 19, 1865. Like the Union soldier, Ellison delivers a message of freedom and liberation, albeit figuratively, in his long-awaited, posthumous novel *Juneteenth*.

This was two and a half years after President Lincoln's Emancipation Proclamation, which freed slaves in states waging war against the Union. The commanding officer of those troops announced to the local slaves that they were finally free. The date is still marked with celebrations and festivities in many African American communities in Texas.

The Plot. The initial event of the novel is an assassination attempt made upon Senator Adam Sunraider, who is presumed to be white, though his race is left unclear. Sunraider, also known as Bliss, calls from his deathbed for a reunion with his friend and surrogate father, the Reverend Alonzo Hickman. Bliss had been abandoned as a child by his white mother and an unidentified father and was raised in a black community. He was exposed to all facets of black culture by Hickman, a jazz musician and later a revivalist minister. Once grown, Bliss ran away and tried to reinvent himself as a con

man and would-be filmmaker. Eventually, he again re-creates himself by using some of his influence to get elected to political office.

Sunraider has become, in his political role, a racist, self-serving individual. Now, faced with the end of his life, he must deal with the hidden parts of himself. Hickman, as requested, comes to Bliss's deathbed and confronts him with his past. The narrative point of view shifts back and forth between Bliss and Hickman as they converse over the course of the story. The conversation between the two men vividly re-creates the events that helped to define each of them, as well as to divide them from each other. The central division is race, but a larger issue is Bliss's inability or unwillingness to accept the part of himself that encompasses being black.

Analysis. *Juneteenth* is clearly an extension of themes present in *Invisible Man* and of Ellison's ideas about the American experience. He believed that society as a whole needed to embrace its black history as part and parcel of its culture. Some critical assessments of *Juneteenth* make the point that Ellison seems to be calling for an understanding of the contradictory attitude that Americans hold toward their mixed cultural roots. Because the United States is partly black, all U.S. citizens may be said to be inherently tied to black culture. To deny U.S. cultural history by dividing it into parts—white and black—is to create an inaccurate reflection of the past and the present. Ellison further implies that, in dividing history and culture between white and black, people fail to complete themselves and are thus prevented from developing a coherent, solid integrity as individuals and as a nation.

These ideas are clearly an extension of the *Invisible Man* narrator's concept that he somehow speaks for us. Not only does the Invisible Man speak for us, but we cannot be "us" until we know him, that is, until he becomes "visible." We cannot be "us" until we understand, as Bliss ultimately does, that the Invisible Man *is* also us. *Juneteenth* builds on the ideas of Ellison's earlier novel but in an even more complex and challenging way. It employs more layers, allusions, stream-of-consciousness passages, and interior monologues. It is more psychological than action-directed, and it depends on free-floating, somewhat mazelike dialogue.

While reviews of *Juneteenth* were mixed, there is no denying that Ellison employs powerful language to deal with mythic themes, such as the biblical Garden of Eden. In one flashback to Bliss's childhood, there is a sense of Eden and its loss, symbolized in Sunraider's first name, Adam. Hickman describes Sunraider's childhood nickname: "Bliss is what he is called because that is what ignorance is." Also found in the novel are themes of finding oneself, of stripping away invented selves and roles such as Sunraider's race-baiting politician, and of integrating one's self with one's roots. Ultimately, the novel is a celebration of freedom, represented by the Juneteenth festival, and of the wholeness that makes up the American cultural landscape.

SOURCES FOR FURTHER STUDY

Cassidy, Thomas. "Juneteenth: A Novel." In *Magill's Literary Annual, 2000*, edited by John D. Wilson. Pasadena, Calif: Salem Press, 2000.

Kakutani, Michiko. "*Juneteenth*: Executor Tidies up Ellison's Unfinished Symphony." *New York Times*, May 25, 1999 (http://www.nytimes.com/books/99/05/23/daily/05299ellison-book-review.html).

Lightfoot, Judy. "Ellison's Second Act, Visible at Last." *Seattle Weekly*, June 3, 1999 (http://www.SeattleWeekly.com/features/9922/books.lightfoot.html).

Menand, Louis. "Unfinished Business." *New York Times*, June 20, 1999 (http://www.nytimes.com/books/99/06/20/reviews/990620.20menandt.html).

Other Works

FLYING HOME AND OTHER STORIES

(1996). This book, due to the efforts of Ralph Ellison's friend and editor John F. Callahan, collects Ellison's short stories, which appeared previously in magazines and literary journals. Both of the early short stories "Flying Home" and "King of the Bingo Game" depict young alienated protagonists who seek to override the stereotypical roles society designs for them because of their race. "Flying Home," set during World War II, describes a young black pilot who has come to hate his own race because of the limitations his skin color places on him. He is injured in a plane crash and is nursed back to health by a group of farmers who help him to get in touch with his sense of culture and recreate his sense of personal and racial self-esteem. "King of the Bingo Game" deals with

The dreams and hopes of the young protagonist in Ellison's short story "Flying Home" are seen in the eyes of these black World War II pilots, the Tuskeegee Airmen. Trained in Alabama, the Tuskeegee Airmen formed the first African American flying unit in the U.S. military.

an unnamed protagonist, like the Invisible Man, who in desperation patrakes in a bingo game to raise money to aid his dying wife. Ultimately, the game becomes a metaphor for his life and his inability to direct or control it.

GOING TO THE TERRITORY (1986). This collection contains essays, speeches, reviews, and interviews written since 1957 and echoes many of the ideas presented in *Shadow and Act*. Again, Ellison reflects on personal influences in his life and gives tribute to his mentors Richard Wright and Duke Ellington.

SHADOW AND ACT (1964). This highly acclaimed volume is a collection of essays that includes academic critiques, reminiscences,

interviews, and ideas about writing. It is considered an autobiographical work that also provides considerable insights into *Invisible Man*. The pieces show Ellison at his best as an observer and commentator. Two essays, "That Same Pain, That Same Pleasure" and "The Art of Fiction," are important not only for their ideas but also for demonstrating influences on Ellison's own writing. Also contained in this collection is Ellison's famous response to Irving Howe's 1963 critical essay "Black Boys and Native Sons." Ellison's "The World and the Jug" defends his ideas on "the proper subject for black writers" in opposition to Howe's insistence that African American authors must write protest novels.

Resources

Below are listed a few of the many resources for information about Ralph Ellison, his works, and critical assessments of his importance as a writer:

Wichita State University Special Collections and University Archives. The Wichita State University holds an autographed manuscript of a speech that Ellison delivered in 1953, "Brave Words for a Startling Occasion," after he won the National Book Award. (http: //www.twsu.edu/library/specialcollections/74-24-b.html)

Special Friends of Ralph Ellison Library. This library, named for Ralph Ellison, in Oklahoma City, Oklahoma, holds activities in commemoration of African American writers as well as annual Juneteenth celebrations. (http://connections.connetok.com/friends/ellison.html)

Literature of Ethnicity. This Web site has links to many other general sites concerned with African American literature.(http://www.salsem.Ac.At/csacl/progs/lit98/group8/B.htm)

Ralph Ellison's *Invisible Man*. This Web site, maintained by a University of Pennsylvania English professor, Al Filreis, features novel summaries, reviews, and the controversial Irving Howe essay "Black Boys and Native Sons," which prompted Ellison's famous "The World and the Jug" essay. (http://dept.english.upenn.edu/~afilreis/50s/ellison-main.html)

SHERRY MORTON-MOLLO

William Faulkner

BORN: September 25, 1897, New Albany, Mississippi
DIED: July 6, 1962, Byhalia, Mississippi
IDENTIFICATION: Mid-twentieth-century American novelist known for his innovative writing style and treatment of provocative themes in a series of interconnected novels and short stories set in rural Mississippi.

William Faulkner's stature is chiefly attributed to his series of novels and stories collectively called the Yoknapatawpha saga, after the imaginary Mississippi county where all are set. The works most widely regarded as his masterpieces, including the stream-of-consciousness novel *The Sound and the Fury* (1929), appeared early in his career before his genius was widely recognized. Faulkner was "discovered" and saved from critical neglect after World War II, and despite the fact that his best work was behind him, his reputation quickly soared. He was awarded the Nobel Prize in literature in 1949 and today is often considered among the greatest American novelists of the twentieth century.

The Writer's Life

At the time of William Cuthbert Faulkner's birth on September 25, 1897, his family had entered a period of gradual but steady decline. Only three generations before, the name Falkner (the novelist later changed the spelling of his surname in an attempt to distinguish himself from his forebears) had been one of the most illustrious names in Mississippi.

Faulkner's great-grandfather, William Clark Falkner, had been a local hero during the Civil War. After the war the Old Colonel, as he was called, built a railroad, won election to the state legislature, toured Europe, wrote *The White Rose of Memphis* (1881) and other novels, and was shot to death by a former business partner in the streets of Ripley, Mississippi.

In 1885 the Old Colonel's eldest son, John Wesley Thompson Falkner, moved his family to Oxford, Mississippi, where he took control of the railroad. He, too, was active in politics, as deputy U.S. attorney, state senator, and city alderman. When he decided to sell the railroad in 1902, his disappointed eldest son, Murry, the novelist's father, was compelled to turn to less lucrative businesses, running a livery stable and later a hardware store. Though Murry eventually became business manager of the University of Mississippi, his adult life was overshadowed by the successes of his father and grandfather.

Childhood and Youth.

William Faulkner was the oldest of Murry and Maud Butler Falkner's four children, all sons. The marriage was strained by Murry's gradual withdrawal into alcoholism and frustrated isolation. Shy and sensitive, Faulkner was at best an indifferent student, dropping out of high school in the eleventh grade and taking a job as assistant bookkeeper in his grandfather's Oxford bank.

Billy Falkner [center] with his three siblings, all boys and all younger: Jack [left], Johncy [right], and Dean [front]. This photograph was taken around 1910–1911, eight or so years before Faulkner changed the spelling of his surname.

At this time Faulkner came under the influence of Phil Stone, a local lawyer with literary interests who urged him to read, draw, and write. With Stone's encouragement, Faulkner contributed sketches and poems to university publications. Meanwhile, after being rejected by the U.S. military because of his short stature, Faulkner volunteered for the British Royal Air Force in Canada. He reported to Toronto for training, only to have the armistice cut short his opportunity for military experience in the fall of 1918. While his military career did not measure up to that of the Old Colonel, it gave him experiences he would use in his later writing.

Postwar Apprenticeship. After his return to Oxford, Faulkner enrolled as a special student at the University of Mississippi, although he did not meet regular admission requirements. His academic performance was erratic, but with Phil Stone's guidance, he read the French Symbolist poets and the early modernists. Meanwhile, he was composing, under their influence, poems that would eventually be collected in *The Marble Faun* (1924), his first book.

By the fall of 1920, Faulkner had withdrawn from the university and was working at odd jobs in Oxford. He continued to participate in campus activities, composing a one-act play for the drama club and contributing sketches and poems to the yearbook. Faulkner worked for nearly two years in the university post office, although his performance left much to be desired, and he was eventually forced to resign. By this time, in late 1924, he had gained a local reputation as a ne'er-do-well.

After leaving the post office, Faulkner moved to New Orleans, Louisiana, for six months before sailing to Europe with an artist friend, William Spratling. The two visited Italy, France, and England before returning to Mississippi in late 1925. In New Orleans Faulkner befriended the writer Sherwood Anderson, a contact that significantly changed the direction of his career.

From 1916 until the early 1920s, Faulkner supplied drawings to illustrate the University of Mississippi annals. This pen-and-ink drawing, *Red and Blue Club,* shows the blues musician W. C. Handy's band, which often played for dances at the university. Notice the artist's signature—William Falkner—on this drawing, made before he added the "u" to his name.

With Anderson's encouragement, he wrote his first novel, *Soldiers' Pay* (1926). No longer widely read, it is important as Faulkner's first attempt to assimilate the distinctive postwar spirit of his generation. In the meantime, he had begun to take Anderson's advice and work on projects drawing more directly on his native region. Back in Oxford, despite having published three books, Faulkner was still regarded as a ne'er-do-well, evidence of a once-great family's continuing decline.

By spring of 1927 Faulkner had begun writing "Flags in the Dust," a novel contrasting Old Colonel's Civil War legacy with the disillusioning military experiences of his descendants in World War I. Published in much-edited form as *Sartoris* in 1929, this work launched a series of books set in the mythical Mississippi county of Yoknapatawpha. Two more innovative works followed, *The Sound and the Fury* in 1929 and *As I Lay Dying* in 1930. While both of these novels received favorable reviews, they sold poorly.

Determined to produce a book that would be profitable, Faulkner wrote *Sanctuary* (1931), whose lurid subject matter generated notoriety and sales. It was followed in 1932 by *Light in August*, Faulkner's first extended treatment of racial themes. This novel, too, added more to his reputation among certain critics than it did to his pocketbook.

Marriage and Supplementary Employment.
In 1929 Faulkner married the recently divorced Estelle Oldham Franklin, who had been a childhood sweetheart. Several months later the couple purchased Rowan Oak, a large antebellum house in Oxford. In January 1931, the couple's first child, a daughter, died in infancy. A second child, Jill, was born in June 1933.

In the meantime, Faulkner tried to supplement the meager income generated by his novels. He continued to work part-time for the University of Mississippi. He also began to market his short stories to magazines such as *Saturday Evening Post* and *American Mercury*. In May 1932, he made the first of many trips to

Hollywood, where he met the director Howard Hawks and began to work on screenwriting for several major studios. He worked intermittently on film scripts during the next twenty-three years.

Artistic Maturity.
Despite Faulkner's difficult financial position and the strain that it—along with his frequent absences—added to his married life, the decade of the 1930s proved to be the zenith of his artistic achievement. He followed *As I Lay Dying* and *Light in August* with his most complex narrative, *Absalom, Absalom!* (1936), a meditation on the history of the South embodied in one family. In *The Hamlet* (1940) he produced the first of three comic novels dealing with the predatory Snopes family, representing the New South. His great period con-

Faulkner and his wife, Estelle, walk down the path outside Rowan Oak, the large antebellum home in Oxford, Mississippi, that they purchased shortly after their marriage in 1929. This photograph of the couple was taken in 1955.

In December 1950 Faulkner and his seventeen-year-old daughter, Jill, boarded an American Airlines plane in Memphis, Tennessee. It was snowing as the plane took off for New York, the first leg of a trip to Sweden where he was to receive the 1949 Nobel Prize in Literature.

cluded with the publication of *Go Down, Moses* (1942), a novel comprising interrelated shorter narratives, including a masterpiece, "The Bear."

Despite his productivity, Faulkner was still unable to support his family comfortably by writing alone. He was forced to continue working in Hollywood, and during these years his collaborations with Hawks included such notable successes as the adaptations of Ernest Hemingway's *To Have and Have Not* (1945) and Raymond Chandler's *The Big Sleep* (1946), both starring Humphrey Bogart and Lauren Bacall. In the meantime the literary critic Malcolm Cowley was preparing an anthology that would prove to be a major turning point in Faulkner's career. This volume, *The Portable Faulkner* (1946, 1967), called attention to the "grand design" of the Yoknapatawpha saga.

Faulkner sold the film rights to his next novel, *Intruder in the Dust* (1948), to Hollywood for fifty thousand dollars, and the film was shot in Oxford. He was awarded the 1949 Nobel

Prize in literature, only the fourth American to receive the prize. His acceptance speech, in which he spoke eloquently of his faith that humanity would "not only endure" through the nuclear age "but would prevail," became his most famous public utterance.

Last Years. Faulkner's increasing worldwide celebrity coincided with his declining artistic powers. His work became increasingly sentimental and repetitive. He continued to receive prestigious awards, but this critical bandwagon was partly due to a general desire to compensate for previous neglect. With *The Town*

(1957) and *The Mansion* (1959), Faulkner completed the Snopes trilogy that he had begun decades before, but neither novel ranks among his best works. Much of Faulkner's time during these last years was devoted to making public pronouncements on various social issues, especially during his tours abroad on behalf of the U.S. State Department.

Years of excessive drinking and reckless physical activity took their toll, and Faulkner was hospitalized several times during his last years. On July 6, 1962, he died of a heart attack and was buried in St. Peter's Cemetery in Oxford, Mississippi.

Faulkner, here, accepts the 1949 Nobel Prize in Literature from King Gustaf VI of Sweden. The ceremony, in which a number of Nobel Prize winners received awards, was held in the Concert Hall in Stockholm, Sweden, on December 12, 1950.

HIGHLIGHTS IN FAULKNER'S LIFE

1897	William Faulkner is born on September 25 in New Albany, Mississippi.
1902	His family moves to Oxford, Mississippi, where he lives most of his life.
1914	Faulkner drops out of high school in the eleventh grade.
1918	Changes the spelling of last name; enlists in the Royal Air Force in Canada.
1919	Enrolls as a special student at the University of Mississippi and withdraws the following year.
1924	Meets Sherwood Anderson in New Orleans.
1926	Publishes his first novel, *Soldiers' Pay*.
1929	Publishes *Sartoris*, his first Yoknapatawpha novel; marries Estelle Oldham Franklin; publishes *The Sound and the Fury*.
1930	Writes *As I Lay Dying*; buys Rowan Oak, an antebellum house in Oxford.
1932	Publishes *Light in August*, his first extensive treatment of racial themes.
1932–1937	Works intermittently as a scriptwriter in Hollywood for Metro-Goldwyn-Mayer and Twentieth Century-Fox.
1933	Daughter, Jill, is born.
1936	Faulkner publishes *Absalom, Absalom!*
1942	Publishes *Go Down, Moses*, containing "The Bear."
1942–1945	Works intermittently as a scriptwriter in Hollywood for Warner Brothers.
1950	Receives the 1949 Nobel Prize for literature and delivers famous acceptance address.
1953	Is hospitalized for alcoholism.
1955	Travels on behalf of U.S. State Department to Japan, Europe, and Iceland.
1962	Is injured in fall from a horse and hospitalized; dies of heart attack on July 6 and is buried in Oxford, Mississippi.

The Writer's Work

William Faulkner wrote in numerous literary forms, using a variety of settings and themes. However, he is best known for the fifteen novels and scores of related shorter pieces collectively known as the Yoknapatawpha saga.

Yoknapatawpha. Sherwood Anderson advised Faulkner to write about his "little postage stamp of native soil": the home territory and people he knew best. Eventually, this is exactly what Faulkner did. Drawing on his family's history and tales he had heard on back porches and hunting trips during his youth, he created a mythical county called Yoknapatawpha. He invented its history and geography, elaborated upon them in astonishing detail in stories and novels written over thirty-five years. This immense cycle of interlocking stories spans nearly 150 years in the region's history, from the early nineteenth century, when the land was inhabited by Chickasaw Indians, to the middle of the twentieth century, as the county became modernized.

Bounded on the north by the Tallahatchie River and on the south by the Yoknapatawpha River, Faulkner's "mythical kingdom" covers an area of approximately twenty-four hundred square miles, with a population of just over fifteen thousand. In the map of the county published in *Absalom, Absalom!* (1936), he wryly identified himself as "sole owner and proprietor." The Yoknapatawpha saga has been seen as a parable of the moral history of not just one northwest Mississippi county but of the South as a whole.

Universal Themes. Given the enormous scale of this story, it is not surprising that there are several inconsistencies of detail. Characters who appear in one tale may turn up elsewhere with a different name or may behave quite differently on different occasions. Incidents repeated in several versions are given different dates or widely varying explanations of their causes. For most readers, such inconsistencies hardly matter because the large-scale thematic design of the Yoknapatawpha saga is essentially coherent and convincing.

It is often said that the Yoknapatawpha saga is a powerful representation not only of southern experience but also of general human experience. This idea is certainly what Faulkner

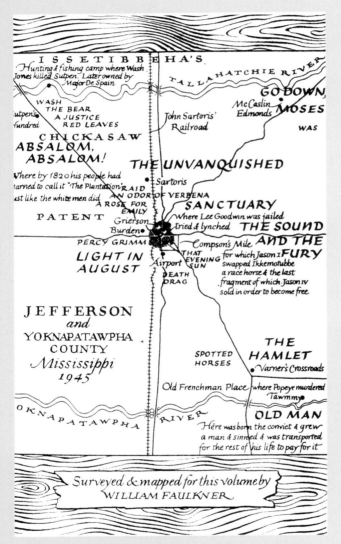

Faulkner drew this map of his "mythical kingdom," Jefferson and Yoknapatawpha County, Mississippi, for inclusion in the *Viking Portable Faulkner,* published in 1946. The map gives commentary about a number of events depicted in Faulkner's various works and indicates where such events took place.

himself emphasized in his Nobel Prize acceptance address, when he spoke of his commitment to write always of "the problems of the human heart in conflict with itself" and of his striving to realize in his fiction "the old universal truths," such as "love and honor and pity and pride and compassion and sacrifice."

Faulkner's People. One of the benefits of setting most of his fiction in the South was that Faulkner could depict a community that was more clearly defined along class lines than is generally common in American society. In pre–Civil War days, southern society was stratified between large landowners, with their indentured slaves; independent yeoman farmers; impoverished tenant farmers; professionals and clerks in town; and poor white and black townspeople, generally manual laborers or domestics.

It was a hierarchical society essentially ruled by the propertied class and the traditional values that codified their elite position. Such Faulkner characters as Jason Lycurgus Compson I in *The Sound and the Fury* and Colonel John Sartoris in *Flags in the Dust* represent this privileged class. Later arrivals in Yoknapatawpha who aspire to such status but use individual determination rather than inheritance to realize it—as does Thomas Sutpen in *Absalom, Absalom!*—embody the southern version of the American Dream.

The Civil War effectively changed the economic structures upon which the power of this elite class depended, allowing others to achieve positions of greater power. Such families as the Beauchamps, the De Spains, and the Stevenses rise to prominence in Jefferson. Poor, unsophisticated farming families, such as the Snopeses of *The Hamlet*, move from the coun-

In a photograph taken in 1938, two African-American women wash clothes in the yard of a former slave shack on a Natchez, Mississippi, plantation. Their younger children play nearby, and eighty-five-year-old Horace Bailey rests on the porch. Although Natchez is some distance southwest of Oxford, where Faulkner lived, the scene is typical of Faulkner's South.

try into the town, where they situate themselves to better advance their interests.

Meanwhile the modern representatives of the old aristocratic families—the suicidal Quentin Compson of *The Sound and the Fury*, young Bayard Sartoris of *Flags in the Dust*—obsessed with their outmoded ancestral traditions, find themselves unable to adjust to changing times. The emergence of African Americans in the South prior to the civil rights movement is forcefully represented by characters such as the ever-resilient Dilsey Gibson of *The Sound and the Fury*, the tormented halfbreed Joe Christmas of *Light in August*, and the proud, stubborn Lucas Beauchamp of *Intruder in the Dust*. Thus, the dynamic metamorphoses of southern society are effectively dramatized in a wide range of characters.

Faulkner's "Obscurity."

Many first-time readers of Faulkner are put off by the oddness and "obscurity" of his writing style. He uses long, convoluted sentences; abstract, multisyllabic words, such as "apotheosis," "immutable," and "relinquishment"; shifting narrators; lengthy flashbacks; and other devices that resist immediate understanding. In this regard his writing style is closer to that of the modernist poets than to that of other contemporary American novelists, such as Ernest Hemingway and John Steinbeck, who generally favored a more ordinary language and straightforward narratives.

Faulkner's style deliberately avoids easy understanding. Instead, it postpones resolution in order to place the reader in a position of intellectual uncertainty until the work has been completed. This reliance on "open form," on keeping everything tentative and in motion for as long as possible, is related to Faulkner's view of time as a fluid medium in which past, present, and future coexist in the mind. As he once put it, "there is no such thing as was because the past is. It is a part of every man, every woman, and every moment. . . . And so a man, a character in a story at any moment of action is not just himself as he is then, he is all that made him, and the long sentence is an attempt to get his past and possibly his future into the instant in which he does something."

Austin Osman Spare's *Dream of Consciousness,* 1955, is a pastel on paper rendering that evokes Benjy's confused ramblings in the opening segment of Faulkner's *The Sound and the Fury.* Thoughts, represented by the split head in the painting, are fragmented, past and present flow and merge, mirroring Faulkner's view of time: the past *is*; it coexists with the present.

SOME INSPIRATIONS BEHIND FAULKNER'S WORK

William Faulkner was deeply absorbed in the life of his Mississippi community, owing in part to his family's legacy. The decline of the Falkner family after the death of the Old Colonel gave Faulkner a keen appreciation of the "old verities" that his and other once-aristocratic families had stood for—courage, honor, compassion, and sacrifice—as well as the realization that such values did not often translate into successful action in the modern world. Faulkner was also indebted to the oral tales of the ordinary country people—both black and white—that he had heard as a child. These tales were full of humor, superstition, and tragedy, recounting in personal terms the experience of the Civil War and Reconstruction, the emergence of the New South, and the struggle over racial integration.

Faulkner's mentor, Phil Stone, encouraged him to read widely in recent European poetry and fiction and to emulate it in his own early writing. Sherwood Anderson, another early mentor, also encouraged Faulkner and gave him the important advice about using his own landscape in his fiction. Faulkner's travels to New Orleans, New York, Italy, France, and England, while not as extensive as those of other writers who lived abroad for long periods during the 1920s, helped to acquaint him with the larger world and with the modernist movement.

His prolonged neglect by critics and the book-buying public was a bitter experience for Faulkner, one that forced him to write for commercial gain in his popular magazine fiction and in the scripts produced for the Hollywood studios. Malcolm Cowley's editorial efforts in compiling *The Portable Faulkner* called attention to the "grand design" of Faulkner's fictional world and to its neglect. The change in Faulkner's fortunes in the years following the appearance of *The Portable Faulkner* and culminating in his receipt of the Nobel Prize coincided with a marked change in his serious writing. His fiction became more affirmative, sentimental, and didactic and less experimental.

A tenant farmer and child stand beside fencing on the King and Anderson Plantation near Clarksdale, Mississippi, a town less than fifty miles from Faulkner's home town of Oxford, Mississippi. This photograph, taken by Marion Post Wolcott in August 1940, captures a view of a people, a time, and a place that was very familiar to Faulkner and to which he was indebted for the color and richness of his stories.

LONG FICTION

1926 Soldiers' Pay
1927 Mosquitoes
1929 Sartoris
1929 The Sound and the Fury
1930 As I Lay Dying
1931 Sanctuary
1932 Light in August
1935 Pylon
1936 Absalom, Absalom!
1938 The Unvanquished
1939 The Wild Palms
1940 The Hamlet
1942 Go Down, Moses
1948 Intruder in the Dust
1951 Requiem for a Nun
1954 A Fable
1957 The Town
1959 The Mansion
1962 The Reivers
1964 The Wishing Tree (fairy tale)
1973 Flags in the Dust (original version of Sartoris), ed. Douglas Day
1976 Mayday (fable)

SHORT FICTION

1931 These Thirteen
1934 Doctor Martino and Other Stories
1945 The Portable Faulkner (revised 1967), ed. Malcolm Cowley
1949 Knight's Gambit
1950 Collected Short Stories of William Faulkner
1955 Big Woods
1958 Three Famous Short Novels
1979 Uncollected Stories of William Faulkner, ed. Joseph L. Blotner

POETRY

1924 The Marble Faun
1933 A Green Bough
1981 Helen: A Court Ship
1981 Mississippi Poems
1984 Vision in Spring, ed. Judith L. Sensibar

SCREENPLAYS

1933 Today We Live
1936 The Road to Glory
1937 Slave Ship
1944 To Have and Have Not
1945 The Southerner
1946 The Big Sleep
1955 Land of the Pharaohs
1982 Faulkner's MGM Screenplays, ed. Bruce F. Kawin

NONFICTION

1958 New Orleans Sketches, ed. Carvel Collins

1959 Faulkner in the University, ed. Frederick L. Gwynn and Joseph L. Blotner
1964 Faulkner at West Point, ed. Joseph L. Fant and Robert Ashley
1965 Essays, Speeches, and Public Letters, ed. James B. Meriwether
1966 The Faulkner-Cowley File: Letters and Memories, 1944–1962, ed. Malcolm Cowley
1968 Lion in the Garden: Interviews with William Faulkner, 1926–1962, ed. James B. Meriwether and Michael Millgate
1977 Selected Letters, ed. Joseph L. Blotner
1992 Thinking of Home: William Faulkner's Letters to His Mother and Father, 1918–1925, ed. James G. Watson

MISCELLANEOUS

1954 The Faulkner Reader
1962 William Faulkner: Early Prose and Poetry, ed. Carvel Collins
1978 The Marionettes: A Play in One Act, ed. Noel Polk

BIBLIOGRAPHY

Blotner, Joseph L. *Faulkner: A Biography*. 2 vols. New York: Random House, 1974.

Brooks, Cleanth. *William Faulkner: The Yoknapatawpha Country*. New Haven, Conn.: Yale University Press, 1963.

Davis, Thadious M. *Faulkner's "Negro": Art and the Southern Context*. Baton Rouge: Louisiana State University Press, 1983.

Hoffman, Frederick J., and Olga Vickery, eds. *William Faulkner: Three Decades of Criticism*. New York: Harcourt, Brace, 1960.

Kawin, Bruce F. *Faulkner and Film*. New York: Frederick Ungar, 1977.

Millgate, Michael. *The Achievement of William Faulkner*. New York: Random House, 1963.

Minter, David. *William Faulkner: His Life and Work*. Baltimore: Johns Hopkins University Press, 1980.

Williamson, Joel. *William Faulkner and Southern History*. New York: Oxford University Press, 1993.

Vickery, Olga W. *The Novels of William Faulkner: A Critical Interpretation*. 1959. Rev. ed. Baton Rouge: Louisiana State University Press, 1964.

The Unvanquished

Genre: Short-story composite
Subgenre: Historical novel
Published: New York, 1938
Time period: 1863–1874
Setting: Fictitious county in Mississippi

Themes and Issues. *The Unvanquished* is made up of seven stories, six of which had been previously published in magazines between 1934 and 1936. William Faulkner revised the stories when preparing the manuscript of the novel, arranging them in chronological order to narrate events concerning the Sartoris family during and immediately after the Civil War. He then wrote an original story, "An Odor of Verbena," which is set nine years later and orchestrates the themes of the preceding stories into a thematic whole.

Thousands of slaves took advantage of the uncertainties created by the Civil War to liberate themselves. Others were set free by Union soldiers as they marched triumphantly through the South. The often confused slaves, traveling on foot or in wagons, headed north. This photograph, taken by Timothy O'Sullivan in 1862, shows escaping slaves crossing the Rappahannock River in Virginia.

This story appears last in the volume and is the strongest. A sort of hybrid of novel and short-story collection, *The Unvanquished* includes several discrete episodes. These are unified by the young first-person narrator and protagonist, Bayard Sartoris; the central focus on Bayard's initiation into manhood; and the moral legacy of Colonel John Sartoris, Bayard's father.

The Plot. The novel begins in the summer of 1863, after the fall of Vicksburg, which, for Mississippians, marked a turning point against the South in the war. Bayard and his black friend Ringo, both twelve, play soldiers, while Bayard's father, Colonel John Sartoris, heads the local regiment. The two boys regard Colonel John as a larger-than-life hero and cannot imagine that he could be defeated. Sartoris has ordered his mother-in-law, Rosa Millard, to have the family silver buried to prevent it from being confiscated by the invaders. The boys take a potshot at a Yankee soldier and successfully seek Granny Millard's protection to prevent being discovered. Later they help Colonel John himself to escape from the Yankees, who proceed to burn down the Sartoris house and set free the local slaves.

Granny Millard pays a formal call on Colonel Dick, a Union officer, and successfully appeals to him to restore the slaves, livestock, and silver that have been confiscated. On the road, she passes a large group of freed slaves headed in a kind of hypnotic trance toward a mythical Jordan. Granny refuses to recognize the reality of change represented by these displaced people and urges them to return "home" to the plantations, most of which no longer exist.

The futility of her clinging to the old order is conclusively demonstrated when she attempts to treat Grumby, a Southern renegade, as if he were an honorable man like the Union officer. He shoots and kills her without a second thought. In revenge, Bayard and Ringo together hunt down Grumby, kill him, nail his body to a door and his severed right hand to Granny's gravestone. Bayard, now just fourteen, is thus initiated into the traditional code of honor that demands retribution for a crime against one's own kin.

When he learns, in "An Odor of Verbena," that his father, Colonel John Sartoris, has been killed by Ben Redmond, a former business partner and political rival, the now twenty-four-year-old Bayard faces a similar

This 1873 oil painting by Julian Scott offers a symbolic abstract of southern types and mirrors the attitudes and values with which Faulkner imbued the protagonist in *The Unvanquished*. The surrendering Confederate soldier is submissive but noble in attitude and bearing. His frail wife and child sit on the road by his side. And standing in attendance behind him is his black slave. He is surrendering, but he is unvanquished because his demonstration of courage brings honor to himself and his family.

test of fidelity to his family and the code of behavior it represents. Pressured by everyone—especially by Drusilla Hawk Sartoris, the colonel's young widow—to shoot Redmond, Bayard decides to renounce violence. He chooses instead to face Redmond unarmed, thereby demonstrating courage and honor without resorting to the bloodshed that had so marked his father's career (and his own with Grumby). Redmond leaves town after the confrontation, never to return. Surviving this test, Bayard has honored his family without sacrificing his principles. He is "the unvanquished" in that he has not allowed the inherited southern code to dictate his actions.

Analysis. In its comparatively straightforward style and clearly drawn characters, *The Unvanquished* serves as an excellent introduction to Faulkner's work. This view has merit not only because of the book's accessibility but also because of its probing exploration of the southern code of behavior—here embodied chiefly by Colonel John Sartoris, based on Faulkner's own great-grandfather—that informs the behavior of many characters in the Yoknapatawpha saga. By setting the action around the pivotal episode in the history of the South, the Civil War, Faulkner enables the reader to understand the origins of attitudes and values whose influence, despite many changes in southern society, are still felt more than a century later.

The southern code is strongly implicated in the violent legacy of the Sartoris family, including its female members such as Drusilla Hawk and Granny Millard. In order to preserve the way of life that the family had epitomized before the war, Colonel John Sartoris resorts to bloodshed and cruelty during the war and its aftermath. He murders a pair of carpetbaggers, northern opportunists who attempt to organize black voters and elect a black marshal in Jefferson. Sartoris ruthlessly kills another man, "almost a neighbor," who had opposed his reelection as commander of the local regiment. He taunts his former partner Redmond after defeating him in a political contest, until still another act of violence results. Although Sartoris's actions are, he believes, necessary to protect his "dream" of preserving the old order, they in effect demonstrate its moral limitations.

Bayard's gradual understanding of the implications of the family legacy is the thematic center of the novel. In honorably rejecting the Sartoris code of violence, Bayard has earned the right to be respected for having the courage to withstand immense social pressure and to follow his own convictions. Yet as Faulkner makes clear in his other novel about this family, *Flags in the Dust*, it is Colonel John Sartoris and not Bayard who is revered as the gallant and dashing Confederate hero by Sartoris's descendants and others in the town of Jefferson. *The Unvanquished* provides a powerful exposure of that myth at the point of its origin.

SOURCES FOR FURTHER STUDY

Brooks, Cleanth. *William Faulkner: The Yoknapatawpha Country.* New Haven, Conn.: Yale University Press, 1963.

Carothers, James B. *William Faulkner's Short Stories.* Ann Arbor, Mich.: UMI Research Press, 1985.

Ferguson, James. *Faulkner's Short Fiction.* Knoxville: University of Tennessee Press, 1991.

Volpe, Edmond L. *A Reader's Guide to William Faulkner.* New York: Farrar, Straus and Giroux, 1964.

Reader's Guide to Major Works

AS I LAY DYING

Genre: Novel
Subgenre: Dark comedy
Published: New York, 1930
Time period: Early twentieth century
Setting: Fictitious county in Mississippi

Themes and Issues. This novel focuses, like *The Sound and the Fury*, on a family in crisis, making use of interior monologues to represent the characters' thought-flow. However, the Bundrens of *As I Lay Dying* come from the opposite end of the social scale as the Compsons. The story of their ten-day odyssey is presented as a dark comedy rather than a tragedy. The novel focuses on the reality of death and the meaning of life.

Addie Bundren, the dying mother of the title, has accepted life as a precious but fleeting gift. In her father's words, "the reason for living was to get ready to stay dead for a long time." Addie's own preparation for death involved the affirmation of love, shared not with her husband, the manipulative Anse Bundren, but with others. It was shared in particular with two of her five children, Cash, her firstborn, and Jewel, the child of a brief but passionate extramarital love affair. Since Addie's death occurs early in the novel, most of the action concentrates on how each surviving member of her family copes with her loss.

As I Lay Dying greatly extends the use of multiple, shifting narrative viewpoints that Faulkner introduced in *The Sound and the Fury*. Here, Faulkner makes use of fifteen first-person narrators, including all seven Bundren family members as well as eight others who observe the Bundren's odyssey from an external perspective. The novel is divided into fifty-nine short chapters, each named for one of the focal characters. The forty-three chapters narrated by the Bundrens tend to be highly subjective and intensely serious; the sixteen chapters narrated by outsiders tend to be more objective and comedic in emphasis.

Nearly a third of the chapters are narrated by the hypersensitive and clairvoyant second son, Darl Bundren. His younger brother Jewel narrates only one chapter, and most of the time we see Jewel as he is seen by other characters, especially Darl. Addie Bundren's one, thematically pivotal, chapter occurs two-thirds of the way through the novel—five days and twenty-eight chapters *after* her death. This deferral, initially disorienting, reinforces the idea of death as a subject of psychological accommodation rather than a mere physiological fact.

The Plot. Addie made a terrible mistake some thirty years ago when she agreed to marry Anse Bundren, an ignorant and self-centered man with a small farm in the hills near the Yoknapatawpha River. Her life with Anse was physically difficult and emotionally frustrating. After bearing him two sons—Cash, now nearly thirty and a carpenter by trade, and Darl, twenty-eight—she made Anse promise that, when she died, he would bury her with her own family forty miles away in Jefferson rather than with his kin in nearby New Hope. Carrying out this promise would, she hoped, make him pay for having duped her with empty talk about a love he was incapable of feeling. For once he would have to do something for her.

Certain that Anse could never connect with her emotionally, Addie had a love affair with Whitfield, a preacher. Jewel, now eighteen, was born soon afterward and was raised as a Bundren. To compensate for Jewel, Addie had another child with Anse, Dewey Dell, age seventeen; and, "to replace the child [she] had robbed him of," yet another, Vardaman, now nine.

As Addie lies on her deathbed, attended by her daughter and a neighbor, her family makes preparations for the long journey to Jefferson. Cash carefully constructs her coffin, getting her approval at each stage. Anse sends Jewel and Darl to deliver a load of lumber in order to earn three dollars. Young Vardaman, scarcely understanding what is going on, catches and guts a huge fish. It begins to rain heavily, and a broken axle delays Jewel and Darl's return; Addie dies during their absence, and her funeral is presided over by the Reverend Whitfield. When Jewel and Darl return three days after Addie's death, the odyssey begins.

The storm worsens until it floods the river, destroying bridges. In a risky attempt to cross at a ford, the wagon is overturned, throwing Cash and Darl into the swirling waters and drowning the mules. Cash suffers a badly broken leg, but Jewel manages to save Addie's coffin. Once across the river, they stay the night at the Armstid farm, while Anse goes into nearby Frenchman's Bend to find more mules. Back on the road, they tie Cash down on top of Addie's coffin, the contents of which have by now begun to stink in the summer heat.

Meanwhile Vardaman confuses his mother in his mind with the fish he had caught and struggles to understand that neither still "is." Dewey Dell is inwardly preoccupied with buying pills to terminate the pregnancy she is trying to keep secret from her family. Cash endures his pain in silence. Jewel, cold and uncommunicative toward everyone else, lavishes his attention on his horse. Anse believes that when he arrives in Jefferson he will be able to buy a much-needed set of false teeth. Darl, preternaturally aware of his family's real thoughts, is the only Bundren who seems to recognize the absurdity of their journey and

Funerals and burials in the depression era 1930s and 1940s were much simpler affairs than funerals today, especially in rural areas. The incidents that occur during the Bundren family's ten-day odyssey carrying their mother's coffin forty miles to Jefferson for burial are absurd. However, the idea of people in those times carrying a family member's coffin over a great distance for burial is not absurd. This photo, taken by Ed Clark, of a rural family in 1940 doing just that echoes the journey of Faulkner's characters in *As I Lay Dying*.

the grotesque spectacle they present to people they encounter on the road.

In the town of Mottson, the Bundrens buy cement to fashion a crude cast for Cash's leg, and Dewey Dell tries in vain to purchase "medicine" for an abortion. Stopping for the night at Gillespie's farm on the eighth day after Addie's death, they put the coffin in the barn because the smell has attracted a flock of buzzards. Darl, observed by Vardaman, sets the barn on fire, but before it burns down, Jewel once again saves Addie's coffin. When Vardaman tells Dewey Dell that Darl set the fire, she sees an opportunity to silence Darl, whom she hates because he alone knows the secret of her pregnancy.

When the Bundrens finally arrive in Jefferson, Anse borrows some shovels from a widow to use in burying Addie. Afterward they take Cash to the doctor, who says Cash will limp for the rest of his life. Darl is seized by two attendants from the state insane asylum, who take him away without protest from anyone in the family. Vardaman eats bananas while coveting a toy train in a store window. Dewey Dell again fails to purchase the pills she seeks and is instead seduced by the drugstore clerk. Anse purchases the false teeth, takes his time in returning the shovels to the widow, and when he finally rejoins his family accompanied by the widow, he introduces them to the new Mrs. Bundren.

Analysis. The choppiness created by Faulkner's use of many short chapters and the countering of Bundren-narrated chapters with those narrated by "outsiders" effectively distances the reader from the main characters. The Bundrens suffer elemental disasters—death, flood, fire—yet ultimately manage to overcome all obstacles and fulfill Anse's promise to bury Addie in Jefferson.

Seeing the Bundrens' struggles both from their own viewpoints and from an external perspective, however, illustrates the ironies of their odyssey. On one hand, the reader is made aware of the ulterior motives behind each character's involvement in the journey, culminating in Anse's triumphant insouciance at the end. On the other, the doggedness with which they persist, despite all odds, in pursuing their ostensible goal is recognized by the bystanders as bizarre and even inhuman in its excess. Such ironies undercut what might otherwise have seemed a heroic filial rite.

The one family member whose sensibility registers the truth beneath appearances is Darl. He recognizes the absurdity of the quest and ultimately tries to bring about its end when he sets the barn on fire. However, his neighbors—and his own family—regard him as insane, a danger to society. The Bundrens' betrayal of Darl parallels their implied betrayal of Addie, notwithstanding Anse's promise. As Cash reflects on Darl in the concluding chapter, "This world is not his world; this life his life." The world that dispenses so readily with Addie and Darl and quickly turns to its own interests is a world that values material things and appearances more than love, fidelity, and the special vision shared by artists and madmen.

SOURCES FOR FURTHER STUDY

Adams, Richard P. *Faulkner: Myth and Motion*. Princeton, N.J.: Princeton University Press, 1968.

Bedient, Calvin. "Pride and Nakedness: *As I Lay Dying*." *Modern Language Quarterly* 29 (March 1968): 61–76.

Bleikasten, Andre. *Faulkner's "As I Lay Dying."* Bloomington: Indiana University Press, 1973.

Ross, Stephen M. "'Voice' in Narrative Texts: The Example of *As I Lay Dying*." *PMLA* 94 (March 1979): 300–310.

THE SOUND AND THE FURY

Genre: Novel
Subgenre: Stream-of-consciousness family history
Published: New York, 1929
Time period: 1898 to 1928
Setting: Jefferson, Mississippi; Cambridge, Massachusetts

Themes and Issues. The novel's title is taken from a famous soliloquy from the fifth act of William Shakespeare's tragedy *Macbeth* (1606), in which it is said that life is nothing but "a tale / Told by an idiot, full of sound and fury / Signifying nothing."

Initially Faulkner's tale is also "told by an idiot," the severely retarded Benjy Compson, whose confused "stream of consciousness" is presented in the first of the novel's four sections. Not only is Benjy unable to comprehend what is happening around him, he cannot distinguish the present from the past. To him, events that occurred thirty years ago are as real and as "present" in his mind as those occurring on the day of his internal monologue, April 7, 1928, his thirty-third birthday. Unable to speak, Benjy can only moan and bellow—the first instance of "sound and fury / Signifying nothing."

Benjy's older brother, Quentin, the monologist of the second section, is obsessed with the past—specifically with the pre–Civil War grandeur of his own family and the chivalrous values his family once embodied. Like the "walking shadow" of the Shakespeare passage, Quentin cannot adapt to living in the present.

His narration takes place on June 2, 1910, the day on which he takes his own life at the age of nineteen.

For the third brother, Jason, life's "significance" is limited to settling old scores and proving himself the only sane member of his family. His failure on both counts leaves him to repeatedly blame everyone around him for his own failures. The fourth section is set during Holy Week in 1928 and contrasts Jason's absurd attempt to recover his fallen stature with the simple dignity of the Easter service attended by the family's loyal, aged black servant, Dilsey Gibson, and her family. For Dilsey, life's "significance" is manifested in divine grace, and the promise of eternity is the agent of time's redemption.

Time is a major theme in the novel, deeply rooted in its structure and characters. The Compson family's past, like that of Faulkner's own family, far outshone its present. Each of the three Compson sons is, in his own way, unable to accept or adjust to this decline. Benjy is unaware of decline and only registers the fact

In Faulkner's *The Sound and the Fury,* the Compson family's aged black servant, Dilsey Gibson, has a strong Christian faith and belief in redemption and eternity. The Thomas Hart Benton painting, *Sunday Morning,* showing African-American worshippers going toward and into a country church captures the simple dignity of Dilsey's faith and evokes her family attending the Easter service at their church in rural Yoknapatawpha County.

of loss, repeated throughout his life but epitomized by the departure of his beloved sister, Caddy.

Quentin's fixation on outmoded notions of female purity and the southern gentleman's duty to preserve it renders him pathologically unable to accept Caddy's adolescent interest in other boys. Jason, convinced that his parents' indulgence of their three older children has cheated him of his birthright, is determined to prevent the same mistake being made with Caddy's daughter (named after the deceased Quentin). Jason, too, is obsessed by a sense of loss, but his reaction is to exact revenge on those he believes most responsible. His attempt to defeat time and recoup loss is, like those of his brothers, doomed to failure.

The Plot. There is little conventional plot in *The Sound and the Fury*. Rather, there is a set of long-standing circumstances that the characters contemplate and react to but do little to alter. They include the death of the Compson children's grandmother, a shared primal experience of loss; the sale of Benjy's favorite pasture to a local golf club to finance Quentin's education at Harvard; Caddy's loss of virginity, subsequent pregnancy, and hurried marriage; Quentin's death by drowning on June 2, 1910, at Harvard; the birth of Miss Quentin, Caddy's daughter; the dissolution of Caddy's marriage and the arrival of her daughter in the Compson household, where Caddy sends her to be raised; and Caddy's secret visits to Jefferson to see Miss Quentin, from whom she has been banished.

In the present, Holy Week of 1928, Benjy is being cared for by a black attendant, Luster, whose only desire is to obtain the price of a ticket to the carnival that has come to town. Benjy is given a piece of birthday cake by Dilsey, Luster's grandmother, and burns his hand on the stove. As Luster puts him to bed that night, they see Miss Quentin climbing down the pear tree by her window, headed for a rendezvous with a man from the carnival. Jason, who has been following Miss Quentin around town in a futile effort to prevent her

from seeing this man, is so preoccupied by this pursuit that he neglects his job and is late wherever he goes. Miss Quentin has found the money sent by her mother for her support and takes it with her when she runs off with the carnival man. Furious at this double loss of income and dignity, Jason chases after her in vain.

Meanwhile, Dilsey and her family attend the Easter service in their church, moved by the sermon about the crucifixion and resurrection of Christ. "I've seed de first en de last," Dilsey remarks on her way back to the Compson house; "I seed de beginnin, en now I sees de endin." The story ends with Benjy howling in protest as Luster drives the wrong way around the Confederate monument in town. Jason arrives abruptly to turn the wagon around and prevent, for the time being, further outcry.

Analysis. *The Sound and the Fury* was Faulkner's favorite among his own novels. He regarded it the most tenderly because the writing of it taught him how best to use his distinctive gifts as a novelist. First, he discovered that he was chiefly interested in the subjective impact of events on the mind rather than in external actions or the analysis of their origins and consequences. This interest led him to the stream-of-consciousness technique, in which the uncensored flow of consciousness is given direct expression.

Second, Faulkner discovered that subjective truth was inevitably fragmentary and relative to each character's interests and capabilities and that a fuller understanding would depend on viewing a composite of several perspectives. Thus, he used multiple narrative viewpoints, from the first-person interior monologues of Benjy and Quentin, to the more public and controlled first-person monologue of Jason, to the third-person, omniscient narration of the fourth section.

Finally, Faulkner discovered that time in the fullest sense goes far beyond objective, or clock, time and subjectively incorporates the past and future into the present moment as it passes. This idea led to his complex deployment of multiple flashbacks within the flow of consciousness and his reliance on repetition of various kinds, such as six-year-old Caddy's climbing of the pear tree to report on the scene of her grandmother's death to her three brothers on the ground below, a recurrent image in each section.

While these methods of storytelling present challenges for the reader, they also avoid lengthy expository summaries and provide apt, economical means of conveying Faulkner's themes. The decline of the Compsons—which is as much moral as social or financial—is powerfully embodied in the utter helplessness of Benjy, the fatal resignation of Quentin, the sheer malice of Jason, and the alienation of both Caddy and her daughter from the family. Dilsey's Christian faith offers a vivid reminder of a glory that has fled from the world of the Compsons and by extension the modern world in general.

SOURCES FOR FURTHER STUDY

Bleikasten, Andre. *The Most Splendid Failure: Faulkner's "The Sound and the Fury."* Bloomington: Indiana University Press, 1976.

Cowan, Michael H., ed. *Twentieth Century Critical Interpretations of "The Sound and the Fury."* Englewood Cliffs, N.J.: Prentice-Hall, 1968.

Kinney, Arthur F., ed. *Critical Essays on Faulkner: The Compson Family.* New York: Garland, 1982.

Matthews, John T. *"The Sound and the Fury": Faulkner and the Lost Cause.* Boston: G. K. Hall, 1991.

Polk, Noel, ed. *New Essays on Faulkner's "The Sound and the Fury."* Cambridge: Cambridge University Press, 1993.

Other Works

ABSALOM, ABSALOM! (1936). Written shortly after the deaths of William Faulkner's father and brother, *Absalom, Absalom!* is a kind of summarizing work. In this novel he published for the first time a chronology and a map of Yoknapatawpha County, calling attention to

The scene in this nineteenth-century Currier and Ives lithograph, *A Cotton Plantation on the Mississippi* (Museum of the City of New York), exemplifies the dream of Thomas Sutpen, the protagonist in Faulkner's *Absalom, Absalom,* to own the largest plantation in Yoknapatawpha County.

his grand design, as well as to that of the protagonist Thomas Sutpen, a figure whose story embodies the central tragedy of his mythological kingdom.

Born into a poor West Virginia farming family in 1807, the young Thomas Sutpen encounters people who possess great wealth and social position. Naïvely believing everyone to be essentially the same, he is turned away from the door of a rich man's house as an inferior. He is so distraught by this experience that he becomes determined to climb to the top of the social ladder and become the master of the biggest plantation around—by any means necessary. Thereafter he single-mindedly devotes his life to accomplishing this goal, a southern version of the American Dream of rising from rags to riches.

Sutpen's rise to power, however, contains the seeds of his eventual destruction. The possibility of African American blood in his family leads to several acts of denial, culminating in the murder of one of his sons by another and Sutpen's desperate search for a male heir who will inherit his immense properties. Sutpen's dehumanizing treatment of slaves and women in effect recalls the act of rejection he had suffered as a child and ironically results in his own murder by one of his victims.

Sutpen's story is told by four different narrators, only one of whom actually knew him: Miss Rosa Coldfield, an elderly spinster who loathes Sutpen for having insulted her more than forty years earlier. Quentin Compson and his father discuss Sutpen's arrival in Jefferson, his purchase of one hundred square miles of

"The Bear," the best-known tale in Faulkner's novel *Go Down, Moses,* tells the story of Isaac McCaslin's crossing into manhood through the ritual of hunting. Arthur Fitzwilliam Tait's 1856 oil-on-canvas painting *The Life of a Hunter: A Tight Fix* illustrates the dangers inherent in hunting a wild animal like a bear and implies the dangers of entering upon the responsibilities of manhood.

land and the building of his mansion, and his marriage and children, as all of these events were recounted by Quentin's grandfather, who served with Sutpen in the Confederate army.

The rest of the story is a reconstruction of Sutpen's downfall, a highly imaginative version on which Quentin collaborates with his roommate at Harvard. The narrative thus involves multiple points of view, repetitions and inconsistencies, and a labyrinthine time scheme. It is Faulkner's most complex novel and, some critics believe, perhaps his most profound.

GO DOWN, MOSES (1942). This book contains seven stories, several of which had been previously published in magazines. However, it was intended to be read as a novel rather than as a collection of stories. *Go Down, Moses* focuses on the McCaslins, one of the leading families of Yoknapatawpha County, from their arrival and settlement in the early 1800s to the 1940s. By far the most famous tale in the novel is "The Bear," an eloquent treatment of young Isaac McCaslin's initiation into manhood through the ritual of hunting.

Faulkner believed that if read separately, "The Bear" should not include the fourth section, which depends for its full meaning on an awareness of the historical context provided by the novel as a whole. When he reprinted "The Bear" as part of a collection of hunting stories called *Big Woods* in 1955, Faulkner deliberately left out this part.

Isaac McCaslin is one of Faulkner's most interesting and elusive protagonists. The moving account of his initiation and especially his repudiation of his birthright in "The Bear" gains resonance when viewed within the larger genealogical framework provided by *Go Down, Moses* as a whole, with its emphasis on such important themes as slavery, miscegenation, and incest.

LIGHT IN AUGUST (1932). The longest and most accessible of Faulkner's major novels, *Light in August* interweaves several narrative lines and frames the central story of Joe Christmas's lifelong quest for identity with the story of Lena Grove's search for her runaway lover, Lucas Burch. The present action spans eleven days in August 1932. After walking all the way from Alabama, the pregnant Lena arrives in Jefferson, where a horrible murder has just occurred. The victim is Joanna Burden, a middle-aged spinster and philanthropist. Joe Christmas, with whom Joanna had been having an illicit affair, has brutally murdered her in an attempt to free himself from the racial and sexual identity she had imposed upon him.

After establishing this situation, Faulkner flashes back to Christmas's youth. Christmas's experiences as an orphan of mysterious parentage, his upbringing by strict foster parents against whom he eventually rebelled, his disturbing initiation into sex with a promiscuous woman—all serve to isolate him and raise insoluble questions about his identity. Though he was raised as a white, Christmas is increasingly perturbed by suggestions that he may be part black.

His life becomes a tortuous journey of search and denial, as he claims and then violently rejects a series of roles imposed on him by religious zealots, women, and racists. As a fanatical Calvinist, a benefactor of black schools, and a sexual partner, Joanna—who assumes that Christmas is black—embodies all of the forces that have labeled him throughout his life and denies Christmas any real opportunity to discover his own identity. Faulkner thus shows the murder of Joanna Burden within the context of Christmas's existential quest. His plight as an individual cut off from the community is given added definition by the presence of other isolated souls: Gail Hightower, a defrocked minister; Byron Bunch, a mill worker; Percy Grimm, Christmas's self-appointed executioner; and Lena Grove.

Christmas's weeklong flight fails to provide any real escape from the environmental trap, and his lynching by a mob led by Grimm only reinforces the racist myths that had victimized him all along. The novel ends, however, not with Christmas's lynching, but with the farcical romance of Lena Grove, on the road again after delivering her child, pursued by another would-be lover.

Resources

Major collections of William Faulkner manuscripts and correspondence may be found at the Alderman Library at the University of Virginia, the Harry Ransom Humanities Research Center at the University of Texas at Austin, the John Davis Williams Library (the "Rowan Oak" papers) at the University of Mississippi in Oxford, the Beinecke Rare Book and Manuscript Library at Yale University, the Howard-Tilton Memorial Library at Tulane University, the New York Public Library (Berg Collection), and the Kent Library (the Brodsky Collection) at Southeast Missouri State University in Cape Girardeau. Other institutions, organizations, and sites of interest to students of Faulkner's life and work include the following:

Center for Faulkner Studies. This organization, located at Southeast Missouri State University in Cape Girardeau, "sponsors and supports educational, research, and public service projects related to the life and work of William Faulkner." (http://www2.semo.edu/cfs/homepage.html)

Mississippi Quarterly. Scholarly journal based at Mississippi State University. The journal publishes an annual issue devoted to Faulkner.

Mississippi Writers Page, William Faulkner. This Internet resource is maintained by the department of English at the University of Mississippi in Oxford, where Faulkner studied and lived most of his life. The site features biographies, articles, and links. (http://www.olemiss.edu/depts.english/mswriters/dir/faulkner_william/internet.html)

William Faulkner on the Web. Probably the most comprehensive Faulkner site on the World Wide Web, providing users with information not only on Faulkner but also on Oxford, Mississippi, on Yoknapatawpha County, on Faulkner's works, and other topics of interest to students. (http://www.mcsr.olemiss.edu/~egjbp/faulkner/html)

William Faulkner Society. Based at the University of Texas at El Paso, this organization fosters the study of Faulkner "from all perspectives and to promoting research, scholarship, and criticism dealing with his writings and their place in literature. The society is also affiliated with *The Faulkner Journal*, a semiannual scholarly journal published (since 1985) at the University of Central Florida.

RONALD G. WALKER

Edna Ferber

BORN: August 15, 1885, Kalamazoo, Michigan
DIED: April 16, 1968, New York, New York
IDENTIFICATION: Early twentieth-century novelist, short-story writer, playwright, journalist, and celebrity.

Edna Ferber's works focus on independent and successful women, the virtues of hard work, and the rights of subjected minorities such as Jews, Native Americans, Latinos, and immigrants. She also chronicles and characterizes regional culture and art history. During her writing career, she gained much critical acclaim, became immensely celebrated, and acquired the Pulitzer Prize for her novel *So Big* (1924) in 1925. Many of her works were made into motion pictures, and her 1926 novel, *Show Boat,* provided the impetus for a long-running and renowned musical. Although her fame and literary standing declined in the late 1960s, she acquired fresh regard from feminists and civil rights activists during the late twentieth century.

The Writer's Life

Edna Jessica Ferber was born in Kalamazoo, Michigan, on August 15, 1885. The daughter of Jacob Charles Ferber, a Jewish Hungarian immigrant, and Julia Newman Ferber, she had one sibling, an elder sister, Fanny.

Childhood. Although Jacob Ferber was intelligent and cultured, he lacked business ability. Attracted to opportunities in Chicago, he sold his business in Kalamazoo and moved to Chicago, where his optimism proved unfounded. He then moved his family to Ottumwa, Iowa, where they lived for seven years before bigotry and anti-Semitism, as well as Jacob's own business ineptitude, drove the family away. The Ferbers then took refuge with Julia's parents in Chicago, and after a period of reorganization, they moved to Appleton, Wisconsin. Here, with support from Julia's family, the Ferbers established a permanent home. However, Jacob's health continued to decline, eventually leaving him blind and subject to periodic severe headaches. Ferber's mother gradually took over the business and became head of the family.

Despite such family upheavals, Edna Ferber enjoyed a comparatively happy childhood and youth. She attended Ryan High School in Appleton, where she wrote for the school newspaper and enthusiastically participated in public speaking exercises and contests. Although she won a scholarship for elocution to Northwestern University, her 1902 high school graduation ended her formal education. Family resources were so inadequate that she had to go to work.

Journalism. Upon graduation from high school, Ferber found a job as a reporter for the *Appleton Daily Crescent* but was discharged eighteen months later. Her departure came shortly after John Meyer, the young city editor and her supervisor, left the paper. His replacement did not appreciate Ferber's overly imaginative writing style and fired her. At this point, thanks to the efforts of John Meyer, she joined the *Milwaukee Journal* as the Appleton correspondent. However, four years later, in 1905, her health broken by overwork and anemia, she returned to her parents' home in Appleton. At this point, with just slightly more than five years of newspaper experience constituting her entire education as a writer, she began writing fiction.

This photograph, taken around 1892, captures Ferber proudly showing off her attire. The occasion is unknown.

Becoming a Professional Writer. Ferber wrote her first short story, "The Homely Heroine" (1910), and her first novel, *Dawn O'Hara: The Girl Who Laughed* (1911), while recuperating from anemia and nervous exhaustion. The novel reached the publication stage only because her mother rescued it from the trash bin, where a disheartened Edna had disposed of it. In 1909, following Jacob Ferber's death, Julia Ferber moved to Chicago with her two daughters. The move enabled Ferber to recover her health, and she began writing short stories for magazines. Of particular importance was "Representing T. A. Buck," which prompted the *American* magazine to request more stories about Emma McChesney, a traveling female sales representative. Although mildly unenthusiastic about the sequel idea, Ferber submitted a second story, "Roast Beef Medium," which launched her popular Emma McChesney series.

Ferber poses for a photograph around 1925, the year she won the Pulitzer Prize for her novel *So Big*.

FILMS BASED ON FERBER'S STORIES

1918 Our Mrs. McChesney
1919 A Gay Old Dog
1921 No Woman Knows
1924 So Big
1925 Classified
1925 Welcome Home
1926 Gigolo
1928 Mother Knows Best
1929 Come and Get It
1929 Show Boat
1929 Hard to Get
1930 The Royal Family of Broadway
1931 Cimarron
1932 So Big
1932 The Expert
1933 Dinner at Eight
1934 Glamour
1936 Come and Get It
1936 Show Boat
1937 Stage Door
1939 No Place to Go
1945 Saratoga Trunk
1951 Show Boat
1953 So Big
1956 Giant
1960 Cimarron
1960 Ice Palace
1977 The Royal Family (TV)
1989 Dinner at Eight (TV)
1989 Show Boat (TV)
1995 Stage Door

New York. Ferber moved with her mother to New York City in 1912 at the urging of her editor at the *American,* Bert Boyden. Her sister, Fanny, had by this time married. In New York City, Ferber and her mother shared a succession of apartments and hotel suites. Periodically, they moved back to Chicago or elsewhere for months at a time while Ferber pursued her writing career. Although she traveled extensively, often abroad, Ferber considered herself first and foremost a New Yorker. Throughout, Ferber's life was dominated by her mother.

Ferber's career as a professional writer brought her into the political arena. She covered the 1912 Democratic and Republican conventions with William Allen White, J. N. Darling, George Fitch, and Harry Webster for the George Matthew Adams Newspaper Syndicate. White, a seasoned newspaperman in his forties, was greatly attracted to Ferber, and they formed a lifelong friendship. Ferber dedicated her second novel, *Fanny Herself* (1917), to White, and White later played an influential role in Ferber's

winning of the Pulitzer Prize. During World War II, Ferber ventured to Europe as a war correspondent for the U.S. Army and was deeply affected by the Holocaust. Much later she wrote passionately of her hatred for Nazi Germany in her 1963 memoir, *A Kind of Magic.*

Stagestruck from childhood, Ferber began her career as a coauthor of plays, such as the popular *Our Mrs. McChesney,* written in collaboration with George V. Hobart in 1915. A second play, *$1200 a Year* (1920), which she wrote with Newman A. Levy, was less successful. However, *Minick* (1924), authored with the renowned playwright George S. Kaufman, launched a relationship that established Ferber's permanent reputation in the theater. In addition, during World War II, the author penned propaganda tracts for the War Writers Board and promoted war bond sales.

In the early 1930s Ferber actively involved herself in the Round Table, a group of writers and celebrities who met daily for lunch in New York City's Algonquin Hotel. Here she met such luminaries as Robert Sherwood, Marc Connally, Dorothy Parker, Katherine Cornell, Franklin P. Adams, and Louis Bromfield.

Natalie Ascencios's painting *"A Round Table Indeed!"* depicts one of the noted gatherings that took place at the Algonquin Hotel's Round Table in New York City. Ferber and playwright George S. Kaufman, with whom she wrote several plays, dropped in regularly to have lunch and partake in the literary banter. Kaufman, a skilled cardplayer, quickly became a participant in the weekend card game as well. Left to right: (rear) Marc Connelly, Harpo Marx, George S. Kaufman, Robert Sherwood, Dorothy Parker, Robert Benchley, Harold Ross, Heywood Broun; (front) Edna Ferber, Alexander Woollcott, Franklin Pierce Adams.

Connecticut. In 1928 Ferber provided her mother with a New York apartment and built her own home, Treasure Hill, in suburban Connecticut. During the remainder of her mother's life, Ferber resolutely maintained this separate residence, lavishing time and resources in remodeling and landscaping the only dwelling she ever owned. Shortly after her mother's death in 1950, she sold Treasure Hill and returned to a New York apartment.

Although Ferber had

HIGHLIGHTS IN
FERBER'S LIFE

1885   Edna Ferber is born on August 15 in Kalamazoo, Michigan.

1902   Graduates from high school in Appleton, Wisconsin; joins *Appleton Daily Crescent* as a reporter.

1903   Discharged by *Appleton Daily Crescent*; joins *Milwaukee Journal* as a reporter.

1905   Returns home in ill health and begins writing fiction.

1909   Moves to Chicago with mother after father's death.

1910   Publishes first short story, "The Homely Heroine."

1911   Publishes first novel, *Dawn O'Hara: The Girl Who Laughed*.

1912   Moves with mother to New York City.

1912   Meets William Allen White while covering Republican and Democratic national conventions.

1915   Terminates Emma McChesney short story series.

1915   First play, *Our Mrs. McChesney*, written with George V. Hobart, opens on Broadway.

1925   Ferber wins Pulitzer Prize for *So Big*.

1927   *Show Boat*, the highly successful musical based on her novel, opens on Broadway; *The Royal Family*, written with George S. Kaufman, opens on Broadway.

1928   Ferber builds home, Treasure Hill, in Connecticut, declaring independence from her mother.

1950   Mother dies; Ferber sells Treasure Hill and moves to New York City apartment.

1952   Publishes *Giant*, her last major work.

1957   Experiences onset of trigeminal neuralgia, a painful nervous disorder.

1963   Publishes memoir, *A Kind of Magic*.

1965   Diagnosed with cancer.

1968   Dies of stomach cancer in New York City on April 16.

---

close, personal friendships with many men, her letters and diaries fail to reveal any serious romantic attachments, except for what appears to have been an idyllic courtship with Bert Boyden, her young editor at the *American*. Sadly, this encounter ended when Boyden was killed in World War I. As a young woman, Ferber actively socialized with her colleagues John Meyer, of the *Appleton Daily Crescent*, and Wallie Rowland, of the *Milwaukee Journal*. In addition, William Allen White was Ferber's close friend from 1912 to the end of his life. Louis Bromfield also remained a close companion; Ferber enjoyed several long visits with him and his wife in France and also records seeing New Orleans with him. Edna Ferber died, unmarried, of stomach cancer in New York City on April 16, 1968.

The Writer's Work

Edna Ferber wrote short stories, novels, autobiographies, and drama, as well as journalism and essays. She shares her most enduring fame, however, with Oscar Hammerstein II for the Broadway musical and popular film *Show Boat*.

Issues in Ferber's Fiction and Drama.

Deeply influenced by Theodore Roosevelt's social progressivism of the 1910s, Ferber viewed herself as a chronicler and promoter of the American Dream. As a novelist, she glorified hardworking Americans who, despite great odds, climb out of poverty. She relentlessly crusaded against unrestricted capitalism and the ruthless exploitation of American natural resources. Indeed, like many in the post–World War I modernist era, she was a pacifist with a permanent distrust of European values and pretensions. The triviality of the wealthy, the nobility of the working-class underdog, and the tragedy of senseless financial ruin are recurring themes in her work. These popular themes propelled Ferber's career and ensured her popularity during the Roaring Twenties, the Great Depression, and World War II.

Ferber was an early champion of people targeted by discrimination: immigrants, African Americans, Jews, Native Americans, Latinos, and Asian Americans. She strongly favored culture over commerce and aesthetics over vulgar display. She persistently advocated and agitated for women's legal rights, particularly in the workplace, although she never involved herself directly in the suffrage movement that resulted in the Nineteenth Amendment to the U.S. Constitution in 1920, allowing women the right to vote.

Ferber's Fictional Characters.

Although Ferber vehemently insisted that her fictional characters and plots were products of her imagination, she received heavy criticism for thinly disguising living people and events in her works. A notable example is that of the actors in the Barrymore family, whom she parodied in the play *The Royal Family*. Arguably, Ferber's fictive characters—such as Barney Glasgow of *Come and Get It* (1935), a humble and rough-hewn man who acquires great wealth through hard work and ruthless exploitation of the Wisconsin forest, and the immigrant character "Ondie" Olszak of *American Beauty* (1931)—could be considered to be based on real-life people.

Most of Ferber's dominant characters are strong, hardworking women of refined taste. They are loyal to their men and children, patiently suffer adversity, and successfully compete in the worlds of business and art. For instance, while Clio Dulain of *Saratoga Trunk* (1941) subtly manages her impulsive husband, she administers his railroad business as well. It

Ferber's popular character Emma McChesney, a traveling petticoat saleswoman, became the subject of her first play, *Our Mrs. McChesney*. Here, in an undated photograph, Ferber appears with coauthor of the play, George Hobart.

is not surprising, given Ferber's background, that most of her literary husbands and fathers are either plodding dullards or unreliable men of grandiose talents and dreams. Charming professional gamblers persist in Ferber's literature.

Several Ferber characters exhibit disappointment when their children either enter crass commercial careers or turn their backs on higher culture. For example, pioneer Barney Glasgow and his son, Bernard, the corporate manipulator in *Come and Get It,* exemplify this literary tendency.

Ferber's Literary Reputation.

The British Nobel laureate Rudyard Kipling praised Ferber's regional historical fiction, and Sir James M. Barrie, the author of *Peter Pan: Or, the Boy Who Wouldn't Grow Up* (1904), praised her short stories. Ferber received a Pulitzer Prize as well as an honorary doctorate from Columbia University. However, although she was once dubbed America's most famous woman of letters, Ferber is often criticized for the uneven quality of her work. Indeed, some reviewers find her characterizations shallow and her stories highly formulaic.

Advancing age and poor health eventually degraded Ferber's work. Her 1958 *Ice Palace,* influential in Alaska's achieving statehood, was dismissed as propaganda. Similarly, her final work, the autobiography *A Kind of Magic,* was disparaged as poorly organized and overly sentimental. By the time of Ferber's death, critical esteem for her work had dissipated almost entirely, and her books had vanished from curricula in English literature.

The women's movement and the emergence of women's studies programs brought a moderate revival of critical interest in Ferber's work in the later twentieth century. *So Big,* for example, was reprinted with a new critical introduction in 1966. Also, civil rights activists began reevaluating Ferber's treatment of African Americans and other minority groups.

Ferber in a photograph taken shortly before the release of *Great Son,* her 1945 novel.

BIBLIOGRAPHY

Angel, Karen. "The Literature of Realism." *Publisher's Weekly* 242 (1995).

Dickinson, Rogers. *Edna Ferber.* New York: Doubleday, Page, 1925.

Ferber, Edna J. *A Kind of Magic.* New York: Doubleday, 1963.

———. *A Peculiar Treasure.* New York: Doubleday, Doran, 1960.

Gaines, James R. *Wits End: Days and Nights of the Algonquin Round Table.* New York: Harcourt, Brace, Jovanovich, 1977.

Gleason, William. "Find Their Place and Fall in Line: The Revisioning of Women's Work in Herland and Emma McChesney and Co." *Prospects: An Annual Journal of American Cultural Studies* 21 (1996): 39–87.

Goldsmith, Julie Gilbert. *Ferber: A Biography.* Garden City, N.Y.: Doubleday, 1978.

Goldstein, Malcolm. *George S. Kaufman: His Life, His Theatre.* New York: Oxford University Press, 1979.

Horowitz, Steven P. "The Americanization of Edna." *Studies in American Jewish Literature,* 1982, pp. 69–80.

Kunkel, Thomas. *Genius in Disguise: Harold Ross of the New Yorker.* New York: Random House, 1995.

Shaughnessy, Mary Rose. *Women and Success in American Society in the Works of Edna Ferber.* New York: Gordon Press, 1977.

White, William Allen. *The Autobiography of William Allen White.* Lawrence: University of Kansas Press, 1990.

Reader's Guide to Major Works

CIMARRON

Genre: Novel
Subgenre: Regional history
Published: Garden City, New York, 1930
Time period: 1889 to 1930
Setting: Oklahoma

Themes and Issues. This novel illustrates the manner in which uncultivated but energetic pioneers tamed the frontier, ultimately to be displaced or diluted by mundane, orderly, more civilized society. *Cimarron* thematically represents the emerging twentieth-century emancipated woman in its protagonist, Sabra Cravat, a woman who builds a career in business and politics and is juxtaposed with her erratic and irresponsible husband. This realistic regional novel portrays Oklahoma from the land rush of the late 1800s through the oil boom of the 1920s. Sabra, the sheltered daughter of an aristocratic southern family, is transplanted from Wichita, Kansas, to the burgeoning Oklahoma Territory, where she evolves into an assured newspaper owner and congresswoman as the new state grows. Although her husband, Yancey Cravat, a flamboyant lawyer and newspaperman, initially guides and molds his young wife, he ultimately deserts her. Nonetheless, she achieves great success. Subordinate plotlines delineate statements against the exploitation of

Honore Desmond Sharrer's 1951 *Tribute to the American Working People* (Smithsonian American Art Museum, Washington, D.C.), a detail from a five-part painting, pays homage to the hardworking American people of the early twentieth century. Ferber's characters, such as those who develop the Oklahoma frontier in her novel *Cimarron*, often let go of the past to seize the opportunities of a more modern society.

Native Americans, anti-Semitism, and discrimination against African Americans.

The Plot. Sabra Venable, daughter of a displaced family of aristocratic southern origin living in Wichita, Kansas, is swept off her feet by Yancey Cravat, a charming criminal lawyer and newspaperman of uncertain antecedents. Yancey makes the run into Oklahoma Territory but loses his claim to a young, attractive woman through trickery. Sabra moves with him to Oklahoma after he sells his newspaper. There the couple take over a newspaper, the *Oklahoma Wigwam,* and join in developing the new Oklahoma Territory. Yancey avenges the murder of his predecessor at the newspaper and later slays a notorious bandit. When a struggling Jewish merchant is waylaid on the street by a gang of drunken cowboys, Yancey heroically wades into the gunfire and faces down the crowd. He also admirably fights for the rights of the Osage Indians.

Sabra and Yancey's son marries the family servant, the daughter of an Osage chief. Although Yancey had encouraged his son in his relationship with the Osages, Sabra finds them savage and threatening. Ultimately, their son gives up his career as a geologist and adopts Osage ways.

Sabra and Yancey's daughter, Donna, returns from her eastern finishing school, seduces an oil millionaire twice her age, breaks up his marriage, and marries him for his money. Sabra feels betrayed and disappointed by her children's irreverence for higher moral and cultural values. At this point, Yancey finds life difficult and absents himself for weeks and months at a time. Eventually he deserts his family and his newspaper. However, Sabra patiently awaits his return and finds the fortitude necessary to develop the *Oklahoma Wigwam* into a dominant metropolitan newspaper, all the while loyally maintaining Yancey's name as that of the proprietor. In addition, she also enters politics and is elected to

SHORT FICTION

1912	Buttered Side Down
1913	Roast Beef Medium
1914	Personality Plus
1915	Emma McChesney and Co.
1918	Cheerful—By Request
1919	Half Portions
1922	Gigolo
1927	Mother Knows Best
1933	They Brought Their Women
1938	Nobody's in Town
1938	Trees Die at the Top
1947	One Basket

NONFICTION

1939	A Peculiar Treasure
1960	A Peculiar Treasure (revised with new introduction)
1963	A Kind of Magic

PLAYS

1915	Our Mrs. McChesney (with George V. Hobart)
1920	$1200 a Year (with Newman A. Levy)
1924	Minick (with George S. Kaufman)
1927	The Royal Family (with Kaufman)
1932	Dinner at Eight (with Kaufman)
1936	Stage Door (with Kaufman)
1941	The Land Is Bright (with Kaufman)
1948	Bravo! (with Kaufman)

LONG FICTION

1911	Dawn O'Hara: The Girl Who Laughed
1917	Fanny Herself

1921	The Girls
1924	So Big
1926	Show Boat
1930	Cimarron
1931	American Beauty
1935	Come and Get It
1941	Saratoga Trunk
1945	Great Son
1952	Giant
1958	Ice Palace

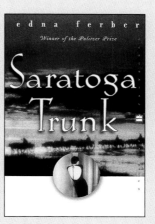

Congress. By the end of the novel, Sabra conducts a tour of the booming oil town Bowlegs and reunites with Yancey as he lies dying after heroically saving the people of the town.

Analysis. Ferber set out to chronicle how a raw frontier encampment is tamed into a settled community. She studied the history and legends of Oklahoma and spent much time travel-

SOME INSPIRATIONS BEHIND FERBER'S WORK

During Ferber's early childhood years in Ottumwa, Iowa, she and her family experienced unremitting anti-Semitism in a rough, marginally impoverished coal-mining town. Ferber recalled desperately running a gauntlet while taking her father's lunch to the family store when she was young. Her witnessing of a lynching deeply impacted the young Ferber, as did recurring violent floods on the Des Moines River. The grim, dull life of the town and the often despondent attitudes of its inhabitants imprinted dark impressions on her imagination that ultimately inspired characters and plot elements in her literary works.

After Ottumwa, the town of Appleton, Wisconsin, was, in contrast, tolerant, comfortable, and prosperous. There, the Jewish community, which included the town's mayor, was respected. In Appleton, Ferber enjoyed about as good and wholesome a life as one could experience in the American Midwest. Ryan High School, a relaxed place where students were encouraged to think for themselves, admired and rewarded Ferber's already developed love of reading and the arts. The citizens of Appleton, from newspaper barons to farm wives, provided a rich source of striking incidents and dramatic personalities for many of her later works, especially *Come and Get It.*

The family store, where Ferber worked from early childhood as her father's health gradually declined, provided a wealth of settings, characters, and dramatic elements. Her experience there instilled her personal appreciation of hard work.

In the animated newspaper environment she entered after graduating from high school, Ferber learned how to observe, how to extract pertinent material from interviews, and, most important, how to write clearly, directly, and objectively. John Meyer, the city editor of the *Appleton Daily Crescent* and Ferber's immediate mentor, along with the newspaper's owner and printer, taught her the newspaper business. In addition, her time at the *Milwaukee Journal,* in particular the tutelage of the sports editor Wallie Rowland, molded Ferber into a talented reporter. Indeed, she identified herself as a newspaperwoman until the end of her life and applied journalistic techniques in her literary research. Her style is arguably that of a newspaper feature writer, and incidents from her newspaper days repeatedly appear in her mature·works.

Doris Lee's 1938 post office scene, a mural commissioned by the Works Progress Administration, a government program designed to help the unemployed, presents the everyday activities that occur at a small-town dry goods store. The spectrum of personality types Ferber witnessed in her family's store gave her much to write about.

ing in the state. In addition, she used her journalistic skills to interview numerous pioneer residents. Ferber claimed that her stories are all based on historical incidents and that her characters are composites of notable figures. Many Oklahomans recognized themselves or their ancestors and were embarrassed by the crudity and violence of some of the recounted stories. Critics argue that although Ferber's stories reflect high melodrama, her characterizations of the men and women who won and tamed the rugged Oklahoma Territory ring true.

SOURCES FOR FURTHER STUDY

Deming, Caren J. "Miscegenation in Popular Western History and Fiction." In *Women and Western American Literature,* edited by Helen Winter Stauffer and Susan J. Rosokowski. Troy, N.Y.: Whitston, 1982.

Goldsmith, Julie Gilbert. *Ferber: A Biography.* Garden City, N.Y.: Doubleday, 1978.

Shaughnessy, Mary Rose. *Women and Success in American Society in the Works of Edna Ferber.* New York: Gordon Press, 1977.

SHOW BOAT

Genre: Novel
Subgenre: Nostalgic romance
Published: Garden City, New York, 1926
Time period: 1870s to 1920s
Setting: Mississippi River; Chicago, Illinois

Themes and Issues. Ferber's recurring theme of heroically competent women contending with less efficient, less reliable men is developed in the careers of Parthenia Hawkes and her daughter, Magnolia Ravenal. The life of Magnolia Ravenal, from her childhood aboard her father's Mississippi showboat through a disastrous marriage to her final status as a showboat operator and mother of a successful serious actress, is *Show Boat's* principal narrative. In addition, the novel's subplots are concerned with the dignity with which African Americans survived injustice in the South. The regional romance of showboat life permeates the novel, making Ferber's story a lasting contribution to American cultural history.

James Bard's 1873 watercolor *Sarah A. Stevens* (Smithsonian American Art Museum) depicts the passage of a showboat on a river. Ferber's novel *Show Boat* offers a rare glimpse of the unique cultural life that existed on a showboat in the late 1800s and early 1900s. This novel, an enduring contribution to American history, is Ferber's most popular.

The Plot. Andy Hawkes, a southern showboat captain, marries a puritanical, spinsterish New England schoolteacher in the town of Thebes, Illinois, on the Mississippi River. Captain Andy persuades his new wife, Parthenia, to give up life ashore and join the company aboard his new showboat, the *Cotton Blossom*. Consequently, Andy and Parthenia's daughter, Magnolia Hawkes, grows up on the showboat, where she eventually falls in love with a dashing young riverboat gambler, Gaylord Ravenal. Because Parthenia violently opposes their marriage, the young couple slips ashore at Metropolis, Illinois, to be married. Their daughter, Kim, named for the states of Kentucky, Illinois, and Missouri, is born near the juncture of the three states aboard the *Cotton Blossom* during a flood.

The Mississippi River represents death as well as birth, as when Captain Andy falls overboard in a heavy fog and drowns. Taking their inheritance, Gaylord, Magnolia, and Kim move to Chicago, where Gaylord continues gambling. Bankrupt, Gaylord deserts his family, and Magnolia embarks on a successful career singing on stage and in nightclubs. Kim, placed in a convent school, is raised as a cultured young lady and grows up to be a successful New York stage actress. Although proud of her daughter, Magnolia feels uncomfortable with the shallowness of her associates. After Parthenia's death, Magnolia returns to the *Cotton Blossom*.

Analysis. Ferber's account of life aboard the Mississippi River showboats, which also operated on other rivers, is critically acclaimed as the single most important source of American popular perceptions of showboat culture and life. Admittedly, lyricist Oscar Hammerstein II and composer Jerome David Kern's immensely popular Broadway musical and film adaptation could rightfully claim responsibility for perpetuating this image in the public consciousness, but both the musical and film closely follow Ferber's plot. Ferber's novel represents the author's intensive library research, personal interviews, and four days on board a showboat.

As in most of her works, Ferber portrays strong, energetic, and competent women, contrasting them with their insubstantial men. For instance, although Captain Andy has good sense, works hard, and knows his business, his wife Parthenia dominates him. After Andy falls overboard and drowns, Parthenia makes a fortune operating the *Cotton Blossom* by herself. Magnolia, although early on ruled by love for her inept husband, illustrates another strong woman who successfully makes her own way in the theater after her husband gambles away their inheritance and deserts her. Magnolia's daughter, Kim, becomes a successful serious actress in another example of Ferber's advocacy of aesthetics.

The entertainer in Everett Shinn's 1910 painting *Dancer in White Before the Footlights* (The Butler Institute of American Art, Youngstown, Ohio) personifies the aspirations of three generations of women in Ferber's novel *Show Boat*, a classic example of Ferber's pervasive theme of strong competent women paired with less-than-competent men.

Show Boat has been criticized of stereotyping in its portrayal of African Americans. This criticism stems mostly from the musical, in which the black roustabouts comprise a happy-go-lucky chorus as the actor and singer Paul Robeson sings the popular "Old Man River." Indeed, although Ferber does characterize working-class African Americans on the river as cheerful, industrious, and docile in the face of physical hardship and prejudice, it could be argued that this portrayal is consistent with her personal advocacy of the dignity inherent in constructive labor. In fact, Ferber's secondary plotline, which relates the tragic fate of an actress, Julie Dozier, a light-skinned African American woman married to a white actor, Steve Baker, dramatizes the injustice and human cost of southern miscegenation.

Show Boat, the musical, which features a libretto by Oscar Hammerstein II, introduced the serious musical play into American theater. *Show Boat* remains Ferber's most popular and most enduring novel.

SOURCES FOR FURTHER STUDY

Berlant, Lauren. "Pax-Americana: The Case of Show Boat." In *Cultural Institutions of the Novel,* edited by William Warner. Durham, N.C.: Duke University Press, 1996.

Breon, Robin. "Show Boat: The Revival, the Racism." *TDR: The Drama Review* 39, no. 2 (1995): 86–105.

Plante, Patricia. "Mark Twain, Ferber, and the Mississippi." *Mark Twain Journal* 13, no. 2 (1966): 8–10.

SO BIG

Genre: Novel
Subgenre: Regional romance
Published: Garden City, New York, 1924
Time period: 1890s to 1920s
Setting: Chicago, Illinois

Themes and Issues. *So Big* epitomizes Ferber's themes of strong, complex, highly competent women who, despite great odds and the influence of ineffectual men, rise to success through hard work. The novel narrates the journey of Selina Peake, who, after the death of her husband, sacrifices herself to prepare the way to artistic success for her son, So Big, and to secure for him a place among upper-class, creative people. However, So Big comes to constitute the other half of the Ferber strong woman/weak man dichotomy by abandoning a promising career as an architect to become a bond salesman. Here, Ferber's themes of the rewards of toil and the achievement of satisfaction through aesthetics are represented. Although So Big makes money and joins high society, he ultimately realizes that he has wasted his talents.

The Plot. Selina Peake, the pampered daughter of a professional gambler, is suddenly reduced to poverty when her father is murdered. Through the influence of affluent friends, she obtains a teaching position in High Prairie, a community of Dutch market gardeners near Chicago. There, missing the comforts of her former city life, she boards with the Pool family.

The maternal figure in Mary Cassatt's *Mother and Child* (Wichita Art Museum, Wichita, Kansas) reflects the strong and nurturing nature of Selina Peake in Ferber's Pulitzer Prize–winning novel *So Big.*

Although her students are initially disappointing, the artistically talented Roelf Pool encourages her and she successfully mentors him.

Soon, Selina marries the widower Pervus DeJong, a well-meaning but unimaginative improvident farmer with whom she has a son, Dirk—nicknamed So Big—who becomes the focus of Selina's life. After Pervus's death Selina introduces efficient agricultural practices that greatly increase the farm's yield. She also successfully transports produce to Chicago, where she establishes herself as a reputable purveyor of quality produce.

Selina sacrifices her own chances of happiness to ensure that So Big is raised and educated for a career in architecture. Although So Big does become an architect, he fails to dedicate himself to his art. After World War I, he undertakes a career in banking, gains a large income, and enters glittering but shallow high society. In contrast, Selina's former student, the humble Roelf Pool, steadfastly maintains his high ideals and ultimately develops into a world-famous sculptor. At the novel's end, So Big meets Roelf and realizes the futility of his life.

Analysis. By juxtaposing the affluent social circles of Chicago, the working-class community of the Halstead Street Market, and the produce farmers of High Prairie, Ferber paints a multifaceted picture of life in late-nineteenth-and early-twentieth-century Chicago. This accurate and perceptive narrative is based on Ferber's autobiographical imprints of her own Chicago life and on her diligent personal research. It frankly relates the city's significant ins and outs, thereby making a lasting contribution to the cultural and social history of Chicago during its development into a world-class metropolis.

Ferber also preaches the higher value of artistic pursuits—in this case, sculpture and architecture—over crass money grubbing. This—along with her emphasis on the virtues and rewards of hard, physical labor—is a recurrent theme in her work. Furthermore, she extols the values of the humble and industrious workers over those of the frivolous and wasteful idle rich.

Finally, *So Big* breaks gender boundaries by casting as the protagonist a strong, capable, hardworking single mother struggling to overcome the handicaps of her gambler father's early death, the torpor of her dull, unenterprising husband, and the disappointment of her son's materialism.

Although *So Big* won the Pulitzer Prize for fiction in 1925, was adapted for film in both 1932 and 1953, and remains Ferber's most acclaimed literary work, it quickly went out of print during her mid-twentieth-century literary decline. Her characterization, critics maintained, was not at all complex, and events in the story were melodramatic and unrealistically coincidental. In addition, renewed interest in the novel, evidenced by a 1996 reprint, suggests more a response to the novel's inherent social message and historical integrity rather than a reevaluation of its literary merit.

SOURCES FOR FURTHER STUDY

Goldsmith, Julie Gilbert. *Ferber: A Biography*. Garden City, N.Y.: Doubleday, 1978.

Mootry, Maria K. "Introduction." In *So Big*, by Edna Ferber. Reprint. Urbana: University of Illinois Press, 1995.

Shaughnessy, Mary Rose. *Women and Success in American Society in the Works of Edna Ferber*. New York: Gordon Press, 1977.

Other Works

GIANT (1952). Another regional historical epoch, the highly acclaimed *Giant* is Ferber's last great work. Leslie Lynton, a characteristically strong Ferber woman who lives in Virginian gentility, finds herself swept off her feet by a Texas rancher. The two marry and move to Texas, where Leslie encounters Luz, her husband's spinster sister, who rules his gigantic ranch. After Luz's death, Leslie proceeds to guide her husband through repeated crises engendered by conflicts between the ranchers and the oil barons. Mexican Americans, displaced from their land by the Anglo-Americans, are portrayed sympathetically. The 1956 film adaptation, starring Elizabeth Taylor, Rock Hudson, and James Dean, overshadowed the novel.

THE GIRLS (1921). This saga, which chronicles three generations of women, aunts, nieces, mothers, and daughters, all named Charlotte, is set in Chicago between the Civil War and World War I. Charlotte Thrift is forbidden by her family to marry her sweetheart, who dies in the Civil War. As a result, brokenhearted, she never marries. Later, her unmarried niece, Lottie, keeps house for her mother and aunt but goes to France during World War I as a Red Cross volunteer. There, her lover is killed before they can marry, and Lottie gives birth to a child. When she returns home, Lottie passes the baby off as an adopted orphan. Meanwhile Charly Kemp, Lottie's niece, who represents the third female generation in this matrilineal saga, rebels against her domineering mother and marries a budding young poet. History repeats itself after his death prompts Charly to live with her aunt and great-aunt.

The three protagonists represent strong-willed women thoroughly dominated by their mothers—a recurrent theme in Ferber's work. In keeping with Ferber's overall paradigm, the male characters enact roles of incompetent burdens, unacceptable boors, dishonest diehards, or nice guys who die young. Ferber details genuine, midwestern, middle-class attitudes and activities, based on her own personal experience and her diligent research. Although this was Ferber's first nonautobiographical narrative, her primary characters remain based on actual individuals. For example, Charly's young poet strikingly resembles Carl Sandburg.

The Girls earned Ferber moderate acclaim, and for a time, she considered it her best written work. It is interesting to note that many publishers refused publication because the novel mentioned an illegitimate child, a taboo subject for literature of that era. Finally, however, Gertrude Lane, editor of the *Woman's Home Companion,* defiantly accepted the novel for serialization. In response, Ferber continued to work with Lane, serializing many subsequent novels.

ROAST BEEF MEDIUM (1913). This volume was the first of three short-story collections to recount the adventures of Emma McChesney, a divorced woman supporting herself and her son, Jock, as a traveling salesperson for Featherloom petticoats. Emma, obviously inspired by Edna Ferber's early experiences in her family's dry goods store, triumphs over harassment from male competitors and taciturn clients unwilling to deal with a female salesperson. However, although Emma is efficient and assertive, her overly sheltered son grows up to be charming, feckless, and unsuccessful.

The Emma McChesney stories established Ferber's national reputation, and the character was the first fictional female businessperson in American literature. Notably, Emma McChesney was socially accepted as a divorced individual at a time when divorce was denigrated and generally considered shameful.

Ferber published two more Emma McChesney collections: *Personality Plus* in 1914 and *Emma McChesney and Co.* in 1915. Ferber herself rated *Personality Plus* as inferior to Roast Beef Medium. After *Emma McChesney and Co.* received less than enthusiastic reviews, she decided to end the series and concentrate on novels and drama instead. She even declined a contract from *Cosmopolitan* magazine for however many Emma McChesney stories she cared to write at whatever price she might ask. Although she continued to write lucrative short stories for magazines for the remainder of her career, short fiction became subordinate to her novels and plays.

THE ROYAL FAMILY (1927). This play, Ferber's most successful, was written with George S. Kaufman. Her first play, *Our Mrs. McChesney,* written with George Hobart, materialized in response to the personal request of

The clan welcomes yet another member in this still from the television adaptation of Ferber and Kaufman's 1927 play, *The Royal Family,* a parody that parallels the famous theatrical family the Barrymores.

actress Ethel Barrymore, who wanted to play Emma. Ferber's second play, $1200 a Year, in collaboration with a lawyer friend, Newman A. Levy, contrasted the life of a college professor with that of a steel-mill worker to make a pointed message regarding the monetary imbalances inherent in culturally enriching work versus hard physical labor. This was not a popular social concern during the Roaring Twenties, and the play failed. Ferber, however, personally felt she gained competence as a playwright. *The Royal Family,* then, presents a slice of life in a theatrical dynasty, paralleling the life of the celebrated Barrymore family. Ethel Barrymore and another actress flatly refused the lead role, maintaining that they were not interested in enhancing or advertising the Barrymores' reputations.

Resources

The principal collection of Edna Ferber's papers is at the State Historical Society of Wisconsin. An additional collection of her letters to Flora McHolley (Collection #99, folder 571) is in the Library of the University of Delaware. Other sources of interest to students of Edna Ferber include the following:

The Edna Ferber Home Page. Maintained by the Appleton Public Library, in Ferber's hometown of Appleton, Wisconsin, this Web site contains a biography, a bibliography, and useful links. (http://www.apl.org/history/ferber/index.html)

American Literature on the Web, Edna Ferber (1887–1968). This site, a set of resource pages on American literature, has an extensive collection of links on Edna Ferber's life and work. (http://www.nagasakigaigo.ac.jp/ishikawa/amlit/f/ferber20.htm)

Fanny Herself. Available on audiocassette, Ferber's autobiographical coming-of-age novel, written in 1917, tells the story of a young Jewish girl who dreams of success.

M . C A S E Y D I A N A

F. Scott Fitzgerald

BORN: September 24, 1896, St. Paul, Minnesota
DIED: December 21, 1940, Hollywood, California
IDENTIFICATION: Early twentieth-century novelist and short-story writer best known for his depictions of upper-middle-class life in the 1920s.

F. Scott Fitzgerald was the laureate of the Jazz Age, which he credited himself with naming. He wrote about the world of flappers and sheiks, the golden lads and girls of the Roaring Twenties. His lyrical prose offered a portrait of this milieu that is at once sympathetic and critical. Fitzgerald's best work has the pathos, power, and inevitability of Greek tragedy. These qualities are most evident in *The Great Gatsby* (1925), considered Fitzgerald's masterpiece and arguably one of the greatest American novels ever written. In his introduction to *The Portable F. Scott Fitzgerald* (1945), the writer John O'Hara accurately summarized Fitzgerald's achievement, calling him America's "best novelist, one of our best novella-ists, and one of our finest writers of short stories."

The Writer's Life

On July 18, 1933, F. Scott Fitzgerald wrote to John O'Hara, "I am half black Irish and half old American stock with the usual exaggerated ancestral pretensions." The "black Irish" reference is to his mother's family. Mary McQuillan Fitzgerald was the daughter of Philip Francis McQuillan, who, with his family, emigrated from County Fermanagh, Ireland, to America in 1843 and established a successful grocery business. On February 12, 1890, Mary married Edward Fitzgerald, a distant relative of Francis Scott Key, whose full name was given to the couple's first son, Francis Scott Key Fitzgerald, born on September 24, 1896, in St. Paul, Minnesota.

Childhood. F. Scott Fitzgerald grew up on the edge of gentility. In 1893 his father became president of the American Rattan and Willow Works in St. Paul, but the firm failed in 1898. Through the next ten years the family, consisting of Edward, Mollie, Scott, and his sister Annabel, lived in Buffalo and Syracuse, where Edward worked for Procter and Gamble. In 1908 Edward lost his job, and the family returned to St. Paul to live on money from the McQuillan fortune. Fitzgerald recalled growing up in "a house below the average on a street above the average." The family moved several times during Fitzgerald's childhood but always remained on or near Summit Avenue in St. Paul, where the mansions of McQuillan and the railroad magnate James Jerome Hill stood.

Education. In 1908 Fitzgerald matriculated at St. Paul Academy, where his academic career began as it would end. He was a poor student but demonstrated literary talent. In the school's newspaper, *Now and Then*, he made his debut with "The Mystery of the Raymond Mortgage." The school's headmaster, C. N. B. Wheeler, who encouraged Fitzgerald to write, recalled that he also

Two-year-old Fitzgerald holding a riding crop astride a hobbyhorse in 1898. The style and quality of his clothing attests to the genteel status of his family at that time.

showed interest in the stage. Although Fitzgerald chose a different occupation, the theater remained a passion and an influence on his work. Three more of Fitzgerald's stories appeared in *Now and Then* before poor grades compelled him to withdraw from the school in 1911.

Fitzgerald entered the Newman School, a Catholic boarding school in Hackensack, New Jersey. The Newman School was close enough to New York City to allow him to enjoy Broadway productions. In his two years there, he failed four subjects but published three stories in the *Newman News*. His experiences at Newman are reflected in the Basil Duke Lee stories he wrote in 1928 and 1929. It was at Newman in 1912 that he met Father Cyril Sigourney Webster Fay, the model for Monsignor Thayer Darcy in his first novel, *This Side of Paradise* (1920), which he dedicated to Fay.

College Life. In 1913 Fitzgerald entered Princeton at age seventeen. Until he left in October 1917, without a degree, he skipped classes, failed courses, read contemporary fiction, and wrote prolifically. According to one account, he claimed that he chose Princeton because of its Triangle Club, which put on a musical each Christmas. Fitzgerald wrote the books and lyrics for "Fie! Fie! Fi-Fi!" (1914), although his poor grades barred him from appearing in the piece. He was similarly ineligible to act in "The Evil Eye" (1915) and "Safety First" (1916), for both of which he wrote the lyrics.

Fitzgerald contributed poems to the *Nassau Literary Magazine*; several of which appeared in *This Side of Paradise*. In addition, Fitzgerald wrote book reviews and published pieces in the *Nassau Literary Magazine* and the Princeton humor magazine, *The Tiger*.

Fitzgerald probably learned little about liter-

Fitzgerald (left) as a freshman in 1913 with two of his classmates at Princeton University in Princeton, New Jersey. The young men are all wearing identical corduroy trousers, jackets, and caps. The caps, worn by all Freshmen, were better known as dinks.

ature in the classroom. He criticized his English professors in *This Side of Paradise* and again in a letter to his daughter twenty years later. His real mentors were fellow undergraduates such as the future critic Edmund Wilson, Jr., and the poet John Peale Bishop. During his college years Fitzgerald read the nineteenth- and early twentieth-century British authors who would influence his first novel.

Princeton's 1917 yearbook said that Fitzgerald would attend graduate school at Harvard and become a journalist. Instead he joined the army and received his commission

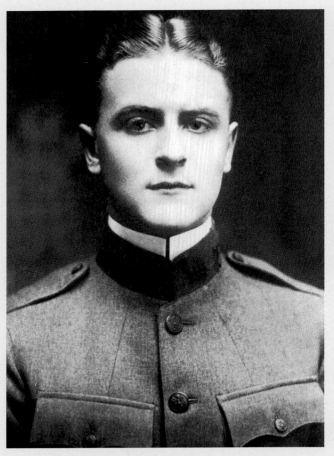

Having had several stories published in prep school and college literary forums, Fitzgerald was eager to begin his writing career. Instead of graduating from Princeton, he joined the army. This photograph, taken in 1918, shows Fitzgerald in his World War I second lieutenant's uniform.

as second lieutenant in October of 1917. He reported to Fort Leavenworth, Kansas, the next month.

The Fledgling Writer. At Fort Leavenworth he began writing "The Romantic Egoist," which would become *This Side of Paradise*. The publisher Charles Scribner's Sons rejected the novel but encouraged Fitzgerald to submit a revised version, which was also rejected.

While stationed at Camp Sheridan, Alabama, in 1918, Fitzgerald met and fell in love with Zelda Sayre. The two became engaged in November 1918, but Zelda wanted to marry a successful, not a struggling, writer. After his discharge from the army in February of 1919, Fitzgerald went to New York City to work for the Barron Collier advertising agency. He wrote

nineteen stories and collected 122 rejection slips before selling a story to *Smart Set* for thirty dollars. Doubting Fitzgerald's earning potential, Zelda broke off their engagement in June 1919.

Fitzgerald responded by going on a three-day drinking spree, quitting his job, and returning to his parents' home in St. Paul. Here he revised his novel once again. Maxwell Perkins, the influential editor at Scribner's, accepted the work in mid-September, and Zelda renewed her engagement with Fitzgerald. In the winter of 1919–1920 Fitzgerald wrote sixteen stories, all of which were accepted in various magazines. "Head and Shoulders," which appeared in the February 21, 1920, issue of the *Saturday Evening Post*, marked the beginning of Fitzgerald's lucrative association with that publication. The magazine paid $400 for "Head and Shoulders," and a decade later it would pay $4,000 for "At Your Age," published on August 17, 1929. Altogether the *Saturday Evening Post* would publish sixty-five of Fitzgerald's stories between 1920 and 1937.

The Twenties. Fitzgerald's first novel, *This Side of Paradise*, was published in March of 1920, the same month that he and Zelda were married at St. Patrick's Cathedral in New York City. Their daughter, Frances Scott, called Scottie, was born on October 26, 1921. Between 1920 and 1922 Fitzgerald published ten stories and another novel, *The Beautiful and Damned* (1922). In another burst of creativity, he wrote eleven stories and seven essays, which earned twenty-two thousand dollars.

Fitzgerald and his wife and daughter sailed for Europe in May of 1924. There he wrote his masterpiece, *The Great Gatsby*. He hoped to begin another novel immediately, but instead the next twenty months passed, in Fitzgerald's words, in "one thousand parties and no work." In December 1926, the family returned to the United States.

For most of the next two years, the family lived at Ellerslie, a mansion outside of Wilmington, Delaware. Fitzgerald made little progress on his fourth novel, wrote few stories,

Fitzgerald, his wife, Zelda, and their daughter, Scottie, do a kick step in front of a heavily decorated Christmas tree. The date and location of this photograph are unknown, but it was most likely taken on their first Christmas in Europe in 1924.

FILMS BASED ON FITZGERALD'S STORIES

1920	*The Chorus Girl's Romance*
1920	*The Husband Hunter*
1921	*The Offshore Pirate*
1924	*Grit*
1926	*The Great Gatsby*
1949	*The Great Gatsby*
1954	*The Last Time I Saw Paris*
1962	*Tender Is the Night*
1974	*The Great Gatsby*
1976	*The Last Tycoon*
1976	*Bernice Bobs Her Hair* (TV)
1985	*Under the Biltmore Clock* (TV)
1985	*Tender Is the Night* (TV)
1987	*Tales from the Hollywood Hills: Pat Hobby Teamed with Genius* (TV)
2000	*The Great Gatsby* (TV)

and spent a brief, unsuccessful period as a screenwriter in Hollywood in 1927. In the spring of 1929 the Fitzgeralds returned to Europe, where Zelda suffered a nervous breakdown in April of 1930, from which he would never fully recover.

The Crack-Up. Although "the Crack-up" is usually applied to Fitzgerald's difficult period of 1935 to 1937, this phrase—the title of one of his autobiographical essays—might refer to much of his entire last decade. His productivity and income decreased as his drinking and spending increased. By 1937 Fitzgerald was thousands of dollars in debt. His last completed novel, *Tender Is the Night* (1934), sold poorly. His fiction began to be rejected by the *Saturday Evening Post* and other magazines, and his accepted work paid less than it had in the pre-depression years. Only *Esquire* welcomed his writing, paying a mere $250 per story.

The Fitzgerald family—Scott, Scottie, and Zelda, holding a large doll—pose on the deck of an ocean liner. They returned to New York from Europe in the winter of 1926. It was during their sojourn in Europe that Fitzgerald wrote his most famous work, *The Great Gatsby*.

Pasting It Together. In July 1937, Fitzgerald began working as a screenwriter in Hollywood for $1,000 per week; in 1938 his salary was raised to $1,250 per week. The money allowed him to pay off his debts. In Hollywood, Fitzgerald began a generally happy affair with the gossip columnist Sheilah Graham, who rejected marriage to an English aristocrat to remain with Fitzgerald. Although Metro-Goldwyn-Mayer did not renew Fitzgerald's contract in 1939, he remained in Hollywood to work as a freelance scriptwriter.

During this period, Fitzgerald experienced a new burst of creativity. In 1939 and 1940 he wrote numerous stories about Pat Hobby, a freelance screenwriter, and he began what might have become his best novel, which he titled *The Love of the Last Tycoon: A Western*. Fitzgerald had completed more than five of the novel's projected nine chapters before dying of a heart attack in Sheilah Graham's apartment on December 21, 1940.

The Writer's Work

While F. Scott Fitzgerald published novels, short stories, essays, and a play, as well as Hollywood screenplays, his best work appeared in his long fiction. His beautiful prose presented the dark side of the American Dream by showing how the pursuit of material success destroyed his characters spiritually and often physically.

Issues in Fitzgerald's Fiction. At the beginning of "The Rich Boy" (1926), Fitzgerald's unnamed narrator remarks, "Let me tell you about the very rich. They are different from you and me." Ernest Hemingway mocked this opening in his 1936 story "The Snows of Kilimanjaro," rejoining, "Yes they have more money." Hemingway's clever riposte ignores Fitzgerald's meaning, which is as much spiritual as financial. As the narrator of "The Rich Boy" notes, money makes people hard and cynical.

In his life and fiction, Fitzgerald understood the value of money. Had he not written a best-selling novel, his wife would have married someone else. *The Great Gatsby*'s Daisy Faye is one of Fitzgerald's many female characters who marries for money rather than love. Money allows Dick Diver in *Tender Is the Night* to build a model clinic.

However, Fitzgerald also knew the price of financial success. He recognized that his best work appeared in his novels, but in order to earn a living, he wrote short stories for magazines that demanded happy endings. His characters, too, sacrifice the best parts of themselves to achieve wealth. Jonquil Cary, of "The Sensible Thing," rejects George O'Kelly until he becomes wealthy; his success earns her love, but their early romantic feelings have died.

Florine Stettheimer's 1921 oil-on-canvas painting *Spring Sale at Bendel's* (Philadelphia Museum of Art, Philadelphia, Pennsylvania) takes a high-camp burlesque look at the life of New York's upper classes. In the painting, chic—and wealthy—shoppers struggle to snatch up bargains at Henri Bendel's, one of Fifth Avenue's fashionable and expensive stores. Stettheimer's caricatural view of the rich evokes Fitzgerald's unsympathetic and sometimes hostile view of America's wealthy classes.

People in Fitzgerald's Fiction. Fitzgerald's prolific output is peopled with a wide assortment of characters, from a ninth-century French knight (Philippe, Count of Villefranche) to an Eskimo, from a southern ne'er-do-well to a European mercenary. However, Fitzgerald's most successful creations derive from his own experiences and social circle, the members of the upper middle class.

Fitzgerald wrote much about the rich, but his hostility to this class barred him from treating them seriously. His essay "What Kind of Husbands Do 'Jimmies' Make" (1924) condemned wealthy Americans as "probably the most shallow, most hollow, most pernicious leisure class in the world." In his magazine fiction he could touch lightly on the frivolity of this world, though even here his animosity is not always hidden. Braddock Washington, who owns a diamond mountain in "The Diamond as Big as the Ritz" (1922), kills anyone who learns of this source of his wealth. At the end of the story, both he and his mountain are destroyed.

Fitzgerald's most sympathetic treatment is reserved for those who must earn their way.

HIGHLIGHTS IN FITZGERALD'S LIFE

1896	F. Scott Fitzgerald is born Francis Scott Key Fitzgerald on September 24 in St. Paul, Minnesota.
1913	Enters Princeton University.
1917	Is commissioned as a second lieutenant in the army; leaves Princeton without degree.
1918	Meets Zelda Sayre in Montgomery, Alabama.
1920	Publishes *This Side of Paradise*; marries Zelda Sayre.
1921	Daughter, Frances Scott (Scottie) Fitzgerald, is born.
1922	Fitzgerald Publishes *The Beautiful and Damned*.
1925	Publishes *The Great Gatsby*; meets Ernest Hemingway.
1930	Zelda Fitzgerald suffers first nervous breakdown.
1934	Fitzgerald publishes *Tender Is the Night*.
1937–1938	Works in Hollywood as screenwriter for Metro-Goldwyn-Mayer; meets and falls in love with Sheilah Graham.
1939–1940	Works as freelance scriptwriter in Hollywood; writes Pat Hobby stories; begins *The Love of the Last Tycoon: A Western*.
1940	Dies of a heart attack in Hollywood, California, on December 21.

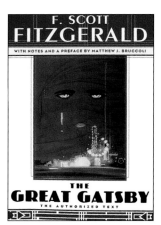

Guy Pène du Bois's 1938 painting *Fog, Amagansett* captures the leisure class, who inhabit Fitzgerald's works. Rich, idle, frivolous people enjoying the good life in an upper-class summer resort town on Long Island. The undefined people in the painting, who appear shallow and insubstantial, mirror the characters in many of Fitzgerald's stories.

Clara Page, a poor widow in *This Side of Paradise*, appears more admirable than the rich girls whom Amory pursues. "Six of One —" (1932) shows that the average young man is more likely to turn out well than those who are "brought up as princes with none of the responsibilities of princes."

Fitzgerald and Film. Fitzgerald spent several years writing screenplays in Hollywood. This work did not prove artistically satisfying to him, in part because he could not adjust to the collaboration necessary to produce a successful screenplay. He received screen credit for only one film, *Three Comrades* (1938). The motion picture industry was more fasci-

nated with Fitzgerald than he was with it, creating over a dozen movies from his stories and novels.

Despite Fitzgerald's dislike of Hollywood, he repeatedly wrote about it, and he adopted cinematic techniques in his fiction. The episodic structure of *This Side of Paradise* suggests cutting from one scene to another. Fitzgerald similarly outlined *The Love of the Last Tycoon: A Western* in episodes rather than in chapters. Its subtitle, *A Western*, proclaims its indebtedness to motion pictures. Fitzgerald's descriptions often imitate a camera on a track, beginning with a distant establishing shot and then moving closer to focus on details. At one of Gatsby's parties, Nick watches throughout the evening a film director bending ever closer to an actress, as though in slow motion, until at last he kisses her.

Literary Reputation. In 1922 *American Magazine* called Fitzgerald "the most famous young writer in America today." The editor of *College Humor* in the early 1920s told the writer Katharine Bush, "What I want is a novel like *This Side of Paradise*." By 1930, though, Vernon Louis Parrington could sum up Fitzgerald as "precocious, ignorant—a short candle already burnt out." Fitzgerald's *Tender Is the Night* enjoyed neither popular nor critical success. At the time of his death, his reputation was in eclipse.

Edmund Wilson's edited version of *The Love of the Last Tycoon: A Western*, published in 1941 as *The Last Tycoon*, began a reassessment of Fitzgerald's work. This critical reevaluation gained added impetus with the 1945 appearance of both *The Crack-Up*, also edited by Wilson, and *The Portable F. Scott Fitzgerald*, with a preface by John O'Hara. By 1968 Richard Lehan could declare that "Fitzgerald is fast approaching a kind of literary sainthood where everything he wrote is considered sacred because he wrote it." In the late 1960s Professor Jackson Bryer of the University of Maryland asked scholars to choose the ten leading twentieth-century American writers. Fitzgerald placed fourth, behind Ernest Hemingway, William Faulkner, and Robert Frost.

Fitzgerald has been regarded by many as the ultimate representative of and spokesperson for the Jazz Age, the name given to the wild and glamorous decade of the 1920s. This 1927 *Vogue* magazine cover not only embodies Jazz Age America but also captures the environment of Fitzgerald's *The Great Gatsby*: high life, city lights, and a glamorous, wealthy flapper.

BIBLIOGRAPHY

Bruccoli, Matthew J. *Some Sort of Epic Grandeur*. San Diego, Calif.: Harcourt Brace Jovanovich, 1981. Rev. ed. New York: Carroll & Graf, 1993.

_____, ed. *Profile of F. Scott Fitzgerald*. Columbus, Ohio: Merrill, 1971.

Chambers, John B. *The Novels of F. Scott Fitzgerald*. New York: St. Martin's Press, 1989.

Donaldson, Scott. *Fool for Love*. New York: Congdon & Weed, 1983.

Kazin, Alfred, ed. *F. Scott Fitzgerald: The Man and His Work*. Cleveland, Ohio: World, 1951.

Mellow, James R. *Invented Lives*. Boston: Houghton Mifflin, 1984.

Meyers, Jeffrey. *Scott Fitzgerald: A Biography*. New York: HarperCollins, 1994.

Miller, James E. *F. Scott Fitzgerald: His Art and His Technique*. New York: New York University Press, 1964. Rev. ed. *The Fictional Technique of Scott Fitzgerald*. Folcroft, Pa.: Folcroft Press, 1974.

Roulston, Robert, and Helen H. Roulston. *The Winding Road to West Egg: The Artistic Development of F. Scott Fitzgerald*. Lewisburg, Pa.: Bucknell University Press, 1995.

Turnbull, Andrew. *Scott Fitzgerald*. New York: Scribner's, 1962.

SOME INSPIRATIONS BEHIND FITZGERALD'S WORK

F. Scott Fitzgerald was above all an autobiographical author. He observed to his secretary, Laura Guthrie, "My characters are all Scott Fitzgerald." The statement is a bit of an exaggeration, because he also peopled his fiction with his relatives, friends, and acquaintances. Zelda and Scottie, classmates, love interests, and would-be love interests appear, often only thinly disguised, in his work.

Fitzgerald was also influenced by his reading. At Princeton, his friend John Peale Bishop introduced him to the poetry of John Keats, Algernon Charles Swinburne, Rupert Brooke, and Paul Verlaine. Among the novelists whom he admired and from whom he drew for his early work are Booth Tarkington, G. K. Chesterton, H. G. Wells, Robert Hugh Benson, and Compton Mackenzie. Fitzgerald was particularly impressed by Mackenzie's *Sinister Street* (1914), initially naming the hero of "The Romantic Egoist" Michael Fane, after the protagonist of Mackenzie's novel.

As Fitzgerald finished *This Side of Paradise*, he discovered the naturalistic fiction of American writers such as Frank and Charles Norris, Theodore Dreiser, Harold Frederick, and James Branch Cabell. The dark tone of *The Beautiful and Damned* reveals this encounter. During the winter of 1919–1920, Fitzgerald first read the work of Joseph Conrad, which inspired his use of the first-person narrator in *The Great Gatsby* and *The Love of the Last Tycoon: A Western*.

Although Fitzgerald recorded the world around him, he also took a keen interest in American history, repeatedly contrasting the gaudy present with an imagined, purer past. Thus, at the site of a World War I battle, Dick Diver of *Tender Is the Night* laments the death of the old order. *The Great Gatsby* ends with an elegy for the America that had gleamed before the eyes of its first explorers.

Although Fitzgerald was influenced by the works of poets and novelists he read and admired, his greatest inspiration came from within himself. Like most autobiographical authors, he drew heavily on his personal experiences, family background, and the social situations in which he found himself. This 1930 oil-on-canvas painting, *Couple Descending Stairs* by J. C. Leyendecker, reflects the partying spirit of Fitzgerald and Zelda and captures the essence of the characters in Fitzgerald's major works.

Filming The Great Gatsby

Hollywood has filmed *The Great Gatsby* three times, as a silent film in 1926, in black and white in 1949, and in color in 1974. In the third adaptation, Francis Ford Coppola wrote the screenplay, showing great reverence to Fitzgerald's text. At times he used voice-overs to preserve Fitzgerald's prose; on other occasions he turned Fitzgerald's commentary into dialogue.

The cast included Robert Redford as Jay Gatsby, Mia Farrow as Daisy Buchanan, Sam Waterston as Nick Carraway, Howard Da Silva in the cameo role of the gangster Meyer Wolfsheim, Bruce Dern as Tom Buchanan, Karen Black as Myrtle Wilson, and Scott Wilson as Myrtle's husband, George. Ralph Lauren helped design the costumes.

The director, Jack Clayton, had been a cinematographer, and his concern for camera work is evident in the movie's lush interiors and exteriors. He used a soft-focus lens, and the pastel colors of the sets and costumes give the film a dreamlike quality. The jazz score, like the costumes and hairdos, rendered a convincing re-creation of the 1920's, and the mansions of Newport, Rhode Island, where this version of *The Great Gatsby* was filmed, mirror those that Fitzgerald described on Long Island.

Critical Response. Given the film's generous budget and its all-star cast, it is surprising that it provoked hostile reviews from most critics. Vincent Canby of the *New York Times* expressed the prevailing opinion in an article titled, "They've Turned 'Gatsby' to Goo."

In part the problem lies with the text itself. Fitzgerald often alludes to situations or objects, where a film must visually show them. For example, Nick hears rumors about Gatsby, but as late as chapter 7, when he goes with Gatsby, Tom, Daisy, and Jordan to the Plaza Hotel the day before Gatsby dies, Nick is not totally certain about this enigmatic figure. Screenplays do not handle ambiguity well. The first time Nick attends one of Gatsby's parties, the novel's Gatsby casually introduces himself. In the film, however, a sinister bodyguard escorts Nick into Gatsby's study, thus emphasizing Gatsby's association with the underworld. The connection is present in the book, of course, but Fitzgerald plays down this side of Gatsby while the film plays it up.

Casting Choices. Many critics noted that as accomplished as both Redford and Dern were as actors in general, the film would have benefited from their switching roles. Redford looks and sounds so polished that it is difficult to believe that he began life as the poor Jay Gatz and that he never fit into the moneyed world to which

This scene from the 1974 color film version of *The Great Gatsby* shows Robert Redford as Jay Gatsby, Mia Farrow as Daisy Buchanan, and Bruce Dern as Daisy's husband, Tom. The elegant tuxedos and glittering gowns capture the lushness and dreamlike quality of this production, a softer and more romantic interpretation than Fitzgerald's novel, which has a harder edge. Sam Waterson, shown in the center of this photograph, plays the narrator, Nick Carraway, who, unlike the others, admires Gatsby. Here Waterson gazes at Redford's Gatsby with sadness, capturing the tenor of Fitzgerald's view of his most famous protagonist.

he aspired. Either the director or the star also decided to make Gatsby more reflective, incorporating pregnant pauses into his speeches. The novel's Gatsby is impulsive and always responding from the heart.

Dern, in contrast, seems ill at ease in his role. Perhaps he is supposed to be feeling guilty about his infidelity to Daisy. Still, his demeanor does not capture the old-money Yale University graduate that Fitzgerald imagines. In the film, Nick comes to visit the Buchanans for the first time, and Tom rides up on a polo pony to greet him. Tom acts like a parvenu, uncomfortable with his wealth. Fitzgerald put Tom in riding clothes but dispensed with the horse.

The Novel's Themes. Fitzgerald was never comfortable writing love scenes, and his novel does not include most of the film's love scenes between Daisy and Gatsby. The subtlety is that Gatsby loves not only Daisy but also what she represents. Nick

Robert Redford as Jay Gatsby leans against a 1920s-era Rolls Royce in this photograph from the 1974 color film version of Fitzgerald's novel.

In this 1968 pastel-and-graphite-on-paper silkscreen print, *Hollywood Study #2* (Anthony d'Offay Gallery, London, England), the artist Ed Ruscha has transported Los Angeles's famous HOLLYWOOD sign from its familiar urban hillside to the top of a barren desert peak. The print evokes how Fitzgerald felt when he was transported from New York to Hollywood to write film scripts: he found the experience artistically barren and unsatisfying.

observes that his distant cousin has an indiscreet voice, full of some quality he cannot name. Gatsby fills in the blank at once: Her voice is full of money, and for Gatsby that timbre is precisely what he admires in her. She also represents Gatsby's lost youth and innocence, and he wants her to deny that she ever loved Tom. He cannot quite believe in her two- or three-year-old daughter (texts differ on the age). He hopes to marry Daisy in her house in Louisville, just as he had hoped to do five years earlier. The camera can caress Gatsby's gold brush and Rolls Royce and lush lawn. It cannot, as a book can, turn Daisy into an embodiment of such possessions and thus of Gatsby's dreams.

Too long by at least thirty minutes—the movie runs two and a half hours—Hollywood's 1974 *Great Gatsby* became an exercise in nostalgia. The novel, too, is elegiac. Nick, the first-person narrator of the story, is looking back on the summer of 1922 with a certain affection, and he laments his lost past and that of his country. Nick, as the novel's outsider-narrator, finally condemns the world of the careless rich. The film is too much in love with its own beauty to deliver that judgment.

SOURCES FOR FURTHER STUDY

Dixon, Wheeler Winston. *The Cinematic Vision of F. Scott Fitzgerald*. Ann Arbor, Mich.: UMI Research, 1986.

Friedrich, Otto. "Reappraisals—F. Scott Fitzgerald: Money, Money, Money." *American Scholar* 29 (Summer 1960): 392–405.

Kuehl, John. *F. Scott Fitzgerald: A Study of the Short Fiction*. Boston: Twayne Publishers, 1991.

Reader's Guide to Major Works

THE GREAT GATSBY

Genre: Novel
Subgenre: Novel of manners; social commentary
Published: New York, 1925
Time period: 1922
Setting: Long Island and Manhattan, New York

Themes and Issues. Ever the moralist, F. Scott Fitzgerald dissects the American Dream in *The Great Gatsby*. Jay Gatsby "believed in the orgiastic future," the promise that if one tries hard enough, one can make enough money with which to buy happiness. Modeled on Benjamin Franklin and the hard-working heroes of Horatio Alger stories, Gatsby becomes fabulously wealthy. Yet he never gains acceptance: He remains Mr. Nobody from Nowhere, as Tom Buchanan calls him.

Gatsby believes that he can correct his past, but Fitzgerald regarded America as a land where there are no second acts. Innocence, he believed, once lost, can never be found again. Gatsby's quest for this impossible dream has a grandeur of its own; the narrator Nick Carraway

This wild party scene from the 1974 movie *The Great Gatsby* shows one of the lavish parties given by the upstart millionaire Jay Gatsby to attract Daisy Buchanan. When she finally does attend one of the parties, the wild abandon displayed by Gatsby's guests repels her, and Gatsby gives no more parties. Fitzgerald uses Daisy's displeasure and its subsequent result to tell his readers not only that Gatsby's parties have ended but that the wild party that is the decade of the 1920s is coming to an end.

declares that Gatsby is worth "the whole damn bunch" of his cynical acquaintances. At the same time, his quest is doomed. Gatsby pays with his life for "living too long with a single dream" in the material world of the 1920s.

The Plot. In the spring of 1922, Nick Carraway of St. Paul, Minnesota, goes east to partake of the prosperity of Wall Street. He moves into a cottage in West Egg, Long Island, separated by water from the more fashionable East Egg, where his distant cousin Daisy Faye, now Daisy Buchanan, lives. One evening in June, Nick dines with his relative and meets her husband, Tom, and their friend Jordan Baker. When Nick returns home, he gets his first glimpse of his neighbor, the millionaire Jay Gatsby.

Over the course of the summer Nick grows close to these characters. He learns that, in the fall of 1917, in Louisville, Kentucky, Gatsby, a poor soldier, had met and fallen in love with Daisy. They were virtually engaged, but while Gatsby was in Europe, Daisy was wooed and won by the wealthy Tom Buchanan. Upon his return Gatsby became an associate of Meyer Wolfsheim, the man who fixed baseball's World Series in 1919. Through bootlegging and forgery, Gatsby amassed a fortune, with which he hoped to win back Daisy. Gatsby buys a mansion across the bay from Daisy's house and gives lavish parties in the hope that Daisy will come to one of them.

She never does, so Gatsby asks Nick to invite her to tea. When Daisy visits Nick, Gatsby walks over and meets her. Gatsby's plan works, and Daisy is impressed with Gatsby's wealth. She attends Gatsby's next party but dislikes it; Gatsby therefore gives no more parties.

On a hot day at the end of summer, Gatsby, Daisy, Tom, Nick, and Jordan drive to the Plaza Hotel in New York City. Gatsby says that Daisy never loved Tom and is leaving him. Daisy replies that she loved them both. Tom exposes the illicit sources of Gatsby's money. Because Daisy wants security above all things, Tom's revelation ends any chance of Daisy's leaving her husband.

On the drive back from the city, Daisy, behind the wheel of Gatsby's car, accidentally hits and kills Myrtle Wilson, Tom's mistress. Myrtle's husband, George, seeks revenge and kills Gatsby, whom he believes to be Myrtle's murderer, and then commits suicide. Nick ends his relationship with Jordan and returns to the Midwest.

Analysis. In the fall of 1924, Fitzgerald wrote to Edmund Wilson, "My book (*Gatsby*) is wonderful." Critics agreed. *The Great Gatsby* is considered one of the greatest American novels, perfect in every way. Fitzgerald is clearly in control of the book's structure. Each of the nine chapters revolves around a party that recalls and comments on the others. In chapter 2, Tom takes his mistress to the Plaza Hotel. In chapter 7, the main characters return there, and Tom the philanderer ironically becomes the spokesperson for marital fidelity. Fitzgerald keeps Gatsby off-stage until chapter 3, heightening this character's mystery. Gatsby and Daisy reunite in chapter 5, the still center of the novel.

At the beginning of chapter 4, Nick reads from an old timetable preserved from his summer on Long Island. The date is July 5, 1922, a sly allusion to the Declaration of Independence. Many of the names on the list—Civet, Beaver, Leeches, Hornbeams, Ferret, Catlips—indicate the animalistic nature of those who prey upon Gatsby's hospitality. Other names recall a purer past: Webster, Stonewall Jackson, Ulysses Swett (reminiscent of Ulysses S. Grant), Henry L. Palmetto. Henry Laurens of South Carolina, the Palmetto State, was a patriot leader during the American Revolution and served as president of the Continental Congress from 1777 to 1778.

The prose here reflects a deft touch. Inside the Buchanan house, Fitzgerald writes, "The crimson room bloomed with light." The verb is at once strange and apt. The telephone rings with "shrill metallic urgency," and leaves behind "the broken fragments of the last five minutes at table." Jordan Baker's gray eyes are "sun-strained." Characters and images leap off the page. It is small wonder that Broadway and Hollywood fell in love with the book and adapted it for stage and screen.

Fitzgerald uses imagery not only to create vivid effects but also to emphasize the book's theme of loss. Every color, for example, degenerates into something other than what it originally seems. White appears to be the color of purity. When Nick first visits the Buchanans, he sees Jordan and Daisy wearing white dresses. The mansions of East Egg glitter in white. New York City rises "in white heaps and sugar lumps." The white New York City is the scene of Tom's adulterous tryst with Myrtle.

Jordan is a cheat and a liar. Daisy will go to the highest bidder. Behind the white facade of their white mansion, Daisy and Tom conspire to send George Wilson to kill Gatsby.

Similarly, green, the color of nature, comes to represent money and corruption. At the one party Daisy attends at Gatsby's house, she tells Nick that if he wants to kiss her, he should present one of the green cards she is distributing. The light at the end of Daisy's dock is green. The first time Nick sees Gatsby, he is reaching out to that object. To Gatsby, Daisy represents youth and the regeneration of springtime, but in the end her green light brings only death.

The color white once represented the snow of Nick's youth; green tickets brought Nick home for Christmas. The green breast of the New World flowered once for the Dutch sailors and filled them with wonder. However, Fitzgerald shows that this world no longer exists. The trees that the Dutch sailors saw have been cut down to make room for Gatsby's house. The fresh green breast of the New World turns into Myrtle's bloody breast, ripped open by a speeding car, a breast without life

---

LONG FICTION

1920 This Side of Paradise
1922 The Beautiful and Damned
1925 The Great Gatsby
1934 Tender Is the Night
1941 The Last Tycoon (revised in 1994 as The Love of the Last Tycoon: A Western)

SHORT FICTION

1920 Flappers and Philosophers
1922 Tales of the Jazz Age
1926 All the Sad Young Men
1935 Taps at Reveille
       The Stories of F. Scott Fitzgerald
1960 Babylon Revisited and Other Stories
1962 The Pat Hobby Stories
1965 The Apprentice Fiction of F. Scott Fitzgerald
1973 The Basil and Josephine Stories

1974 Bits of Paradise
1979 The Price Was High: The Last Uncollected Stories of F. Scott Fitzgerald

PLAY

1923 The Vegetable: Or, From President to Postman

SCREENPLAY

1938 Three Comrades

NONFICTION

1945 The Crack-Up, ed. Edmond Wilson
1963 The Letters of F. Scott Fitzgerald
1965 Letters to His Daughter
1965 Thoughtbook of Francis Scott Fitzgerald
1971 Dear Scott/Dear Max: The Fitzgerald-Perkins Correspondence
1972 As Ever, Scott Fitzgerald
1972 F. Scott Fitzgerald's

Ledger
1978 The Notebooks of F. Scott Fitzgerald
1996 F. Scott Fitzgerald on Authorship

MISCELLANEOUS

1945 The Portable F. Scott Fitzgerald
1958 Afternoon of an Author: A Selection of Uncollected Stories and Essays

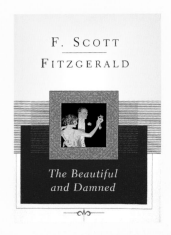

F. SCOTT FITZGERALD

The Beautiful and Damned

beneath it. The 1920s would roar on for another five years, but in *The Great Gatsby*, Fitzgerald had already sung its elegy.

SOURCES FOR FURTHER STUDY

Berman, Ronald. *"The Great Gatsby" and Modern Times.* Urbana: University of Illinois Press, 1994.

Bruccoli, Matthew J., ed. *New Essays on "The Great Gatsby."* Cambridge, England: Cambridge University Press, 1985.

Pendleton, Thomas A. *"I'm Sorry About the Clock": Chronology, Composition, and Narrative Technique in "The Great Gatsby."* Selinsgrove, Pa.: Susquehanna University Press, 1993.

TENDER IS THE NIGHT

Genre: Novel
Subgenre: Domestic fiction
Published: New York, 1934
Time period: 1917–1929
Setting: France; Italy

Themes and Issues. In a 1932 note, Fitzgerald wrote that his novel in progress should illustrate a naturally idealistic man who gives in to bourgeois ideas in his rise to the top of the social world, loses his idealism and talent, and turns to drink and dissipation. As so often in Fitzgerald's fiction, money is the root of evil.

The novel might be subtitled "Portrait of a Marriage." In 1932 Zelda Fitzgerald published *Save Me the Waltz*, about a dancer and her unfaithful, unsympathetic husband. Many of the incidents in that book reappear in *Tender Is the Night* with a slant that makes the male character more sympathetic. The novel suggests how Fitzgerald saw himself, Zelda, and their marriage in the aftermath of Zelda's 1924 affair with a French naval aviator and her nervous breakdown in 1930.

The Plot. Dick Diver, a Rhodes scholar who attended Yale University and Johns Hopkins University, dreams of becoming the world's greatest psychologist. He travels to Vienna to meet Sigmund Freud, the founder of psychoanalysis, and then to Zurich for further study at the Swiss university. Shortly before Diver accepts a commission in the U.S. Army, he meets the wealthy Nicole Warren, who has suffered a nervous breakdown after being sexually abused by her father.

During the war, Nicole writes to Diver in France, and their correspondence helps her to recover her sanity. Diver and Nicole fall in love through their letters, and when Diver is discharged, they are married. Although Diver had planned to write a compendium of psychological ailments, he instead devotes himself to his wife, whose money eliminates any need for him to practice medicine or struggle with his research.

Nicole's money pays for a clinic in Zurich to be run by Diver and a colleague, but Diver is often absent. The Divers establish a summer colony on the Riviera at a time when the fashionable go to more northern beaches to escape

The juxtaposition of simplicity and wealth in this photograph from the 1961 film version of *Tender Is the Night* exemplifies Fitzgerald's theme of an idealistic scholar whose hopes of becoming a great psychologist are ruined by money and a rise in social position.

the heat. In 1925 the actress Rosemary Hoyt comes to the south of France and falls in love with Diver. At first he resists her advances, but after Nicole suffers a second breakdown, Diver, returning from his father's funeral in the United States, seeks out Rosemary in Rome and consummates their affair.

Diver's inability to control his drinking prompts his colleague to dissolve their partnership. Diver returns to Nicole too late to save their marriage. She begins her own affair with the soldier of fortune Tommy Barban. At the end of the book, Diver returns to upstate New York to practice general medicine and to write his book, but his drinking and philandering force him to move from one village to another. Although he survives physically, he is ruined spiritually and intellectually.

Analysis. Although this novel is set largely in the 1920s, it views this era through the jaundiced eyes of the Great Depression of the 1930s. *Tender Is the Night* uses sexual and national ambiguity to show a world gone awry. Lady Caroline Sibley-Biers and Mary North Minghetti disguise themselves as sailors to pick up women. Nicole makes swimming trunks for her husband that look like black lace undergarments.

Tommy Barban reads the names of the people who register at the Hotel Palace at Vevey. Like the list of Gatsby's guests, this one provides humor but also indicates the loss of a stable past. First names and last seem entwined by violence: Moises Teubel, Apostle Alexandre, Seraphim Tullio. Mary Abrams's name sounds Jewish, but she is not Jewish. Mary North's second husband, Minghetti, is not an Italian but a Hindu. Tommy Barban is one-half American, one-half French. He has been educated in France and has served in the armies of eight different countries.

Diver is supposed to be destroyed by his surrender to the Warren money and his devotion to the new world chaos. His disintegration is not, however, totally credible. He does not seem to be as spiritually ruined as Fitzgerald claims. In one of the novel's last scenes, Diver goes out in the middle of the night to help Lady Caroline Sibley-Biers and Mary North Minghetti even though he dislikes them. Although he leaves Nicole, he still cares for her deeply. It is unclear whether wealth should drive Diver to drink and dissipation.

Tender Is the Night contains much fine writing and many memorable portraits. However, it could be argued that Fitzgerald was too emotionally close to his main character to treat him objectively, and the result is a flawed masterpiece, though a masterpiece nonetheless.

SOURCES FOR FURTHER STUDY

Bruccoli, Matthew J., and Judith S. Baughman. *Reader's Companion to F. Scott Fitzgerald's "Tender Is the Night."* Columbia: University of South Carolina Press, 1996.

Stern, Milton R. *"Tender Is the Night": The Broken Universe.* New York: Twayne Publishers, 1994.

Stern, Milton R., ed. *Critical Essays on F. Scott Fitzgerald's "Tender Is the Night."* Boston: G. K. Hall, 1986.

THIS SIDE OF PARADISE
Genre: Novel
Subgenre: *Bildungsroman*
Published: New York, 1920
Time period: 1911–1919
Setting: Princeton and Atlantic City, New Jersey; New York City

Themes and Issues. *This Side of Paradise* focuses on Amory Blaine's life at Princeton University and offers a serious treatment of college life. Although it is suffused with romanticism, the work realistically portrays the experience of adolescence among the wealthy. Fitzgerald's heroines reveal the privileges and problems of liberated women. Unlike their mothers, they are free to kiss and be kissed. Yet they remain unable to earn their own way and so face the same need to marry well, that controlled the lives of their mothers.

The Plot. Amory Blaine travels about the country with his indulgent mother, Beatrice. In 1911 he enters St. Regis, a preparatory school where he becomes a star quarterback and editor of the school newspaper. Two years later he

This panoramic view shows Princeton University in Princeton, New Jersey, as it looked at the time Fitzgerald's protagonist in *This Side of Paradise* was a student there. The stately buildings, with well-kept lawns and well-swept walks, reflect the gracious atmosphere that surrounded the children of wealth attending this Ivy League college.

enrolls at Princeton University, where he joins the theatrical Triangle Club and the editorial board of the *Princetonian*.

During his sophomore Christmas vacation, Amory falls in love with Isabelle Borgé, the first of his three love interests in the novel. The relationship collapses, Amory fails an exam and is barred from holding any posts at Princeton, and the death of Amory's father reveals that the family fortune has dwindled.

Upon graduation from college, Amory serves in the army. At the end of World War I, Amory is destitute and his mother is dead. He takes an apartment in New York City with two former classmates. Amory falls in love with Rosemary Connage, sister of one of his roommates. Because Amory has no money and no prospects, Rosemary rejects him for Dawson Ryder.

Devastated, Amory quits his job, gets drunk, and goes to Maryland to visit an uncle. There he meets the aptly named Eleanor Savage, a romantic free spirit who proves too wild for him. At the end of the novel, Amory is disillusioned with himself and his world. Yet he believes that he has discovered his true self and resolves to continue his struggle for some form of success.

Analysis. *This Side of Paradise* is in many ways an apprentice work. Fitzgerald included in the novel many of the poems and stories he had written in college. The episodic nature of the narrative can be confusing, and Fitzgerald never resolves Amory's ambivalence toward the past. Amory submits a poem in his Princeton English class that rejects and condemns the Victorians. At the same time, he is repulsed by Eleanor's modernity. Amory's assertion of self-knowledge at the end of the novel therefore rings somewhat hollow.

The novel does, however, contain many strengths. It includes passages as lyrical as any in Fitzgerald's more mature fiction. Footsteps sound like "slow dripping." On a spring day in New York City, the air "is a soft light wine." In Maryland, Amory comes upon "wind-drunk trees." The novel handles dialogue with assurance, a consequence of Fitzgerald's close reading of Oscar Wilde and George Bernard Shaw and writing his own plays.

Fitzgerald also introduces the note of sadness that will pervade all of his best writing. Isabelle tells Amory, "I love you—now." Rosalind recognizes that "beauty means the scent of roses and then the death of roses." Amory loses his fortune; his parents and mentor die; love fades. Because Amory emerges from his experiences still believing in himself and his future, this is Fitzgerald's most optimistic novel. Even in this first novel, though, the dream carries a price, one that in later books will prove to be too high.

SOURCES FOR FURTHER STUDY

Hendriksen, Jack. *"This Side of Paradise" as a Bildungsroman.* New York: Peter Lang, 1993.

Stern, Milton R. *The Golden Moment: The Novels of F. Scott Fitzgerald.* Urbana: University of Illinois Press, 1970.

West, James L. W., III. *The Making of "This Side of Paradise."* Philadelphia: University of Pennsylvania Press, 1983.

Other Works

THE BEAUTIFUL AND DAMNED (1922).

Influenced by the naturalism of Theodore Dreiser, Frank and Charles Norris, and George Jean Nathan, F. Scott Fitzgerald presents the story of the disintegration of the marriage of Anthony and Gloria Patch. After graduating from Harvard University, Anthony, the grandson of the very rich Adam Patch, plans to write a history of the Middle Ages. However, he does nothing. A classmate, Dick Caramel, introduces Anthony to his beautiful cousin, Gloria Gilbert. The two marry and indulge in the drunken, extravagant life that marked the Fitzgeralds' behavior. Fitzgerald even assigned parts of Zelda's diary to Gloria.

Disgusted by his grandson's behavior, Adam disinherits Anthony. Fitzgerald here implies that the America of the 1920s has lost its innocence by rejecting its past. Anthony and Gloria contest the will and eventually win the case. However, their victory proves hollow. Anthony is physically and mentally exhausted. Gloria, who has lived only for her beauty, discovers that she is growing old and is, in her view, no longer attractive.

The novel's epigraph reads, "The victor belongs to the spoils." As in many of his other works, Fitzgerald demonstrates the corrupting influence of money, especially unearned money. The Patches are sterile; Gloria is horrified to think she might be pregnant and relieved when she learns she is not, so she can return to her irresponsible life. Indeed, these characters are hardly human. Fitzgerald describes them as resembling "heavily enamelled little figures secure beyond enjoyment." The hope that ends *This Side of Paradise* here turns to despair.

THE LAST TYCOON (1941).

When Fitzgerald first went to Hollywood in 1927, he was unimpressed with Irving Grant Thalberg, then the second vice president and supervisor of production for Metro-Goldwyn-Mayer. A decade later, after Thalberg's 1936 death at the age of thirty-seven, Fitzgerald returned to Hollywood and saw how conditions at Metro-Goldwyn-Mayer had deteriorated. While not blind to Thalberg's flaws, Fitzgerald in his unfinished novel sought to create a sympathetic portrayal of Thalberg in the book's fictional hero, Monroe Stahr.

Fitzgerald recognized the success of *The Great Gatsby* and intended to use it as a model for the work he titled *The Love of the Last Tycoon: A Western.* Like *The Great Gatsby*, it was to be a short novel, containing nine chapters and employing a first-person narrator, in this case Cecelia Brady, the daughter of Stahr's rival, Pat Brady, who is herself in love with Stahr.

Stahr is to be admired for his embrace of traditional American values. Fitzgerald refers to various presidents, especially Lincoln, to emphasize Stahr's association with the past. Stahr also believes in his medium. When a black fisherman says that he never goes to the movies because they have nothing to offer him, Stahr rethinks his projects. His integrity alienates him from the studio's owners, because he cares more for art than money. The communist union organizers also dislike him because of the demands he places on his writers. Fitzgerald understood that Stahr's dedication to excellence exacted a price. Stahr cannot commit himself to either of the women in his life: to Cecilia or to Kathleen Moore.

In *This Side of Paradise* Fitzgerald distinguishes between the hollow "personality" and the "personage" who has heroic qualities. Despite his limitations, Stahr is a personage surrounded by personalities, a true American hero.

The Last Tycoon was edited and published in its unfinished form in 1941 by Fitzgerald's college friend, the critic Edmund Wilson. It earned critical praise from such noted authors as John Dos Passos and Stephen Vincent Benét. In 1994 Fitzgerald's latest working drafts were reedited by the Fitzgerald scholar Matthew J. Bruccoli, to more closely reflect the author's writing process, and published under Fitzgerald's chosen title, *The Love of the Last Tycoon: A Western.*

The film *The Last Tycoon* was based on Fitzgerald's unfinished novel *The Love of the Last Tycoon: A Western.* This 1976 photograph shows Robert De Niro playing the novel's hero, Monroe Stahr, a character Fitzgerald based on Hollywood movie producer Irving Thalberg.

Resources

The F. Scott Fitzgerald Papers are archived in the Manuscripts Division of the Princeton University Library. The collection includes manuscripts of all Fitzgerald's major literary works, as well as related documents and correspondence. Other sources of information for students of F. Scott Fitzgerald include the following:

University of South Carolina at Columbia. The Matthew J. and Arlyn Bruccoli Collection at the Thomas Cooper Library contains more than ten thousand items, including manuscripts, typescripts, the only unrevised galleys of *The Great Gatsby*, books, and such memorabilia as Fitzgerald's commission as a second lieutenant in the U.S. Army. Also housed there are letters, books, and Zelda Fitzgerald's manuscripts.
(http://www.sc.edu.fitzgerald/collection.html)

F. Scott Fitzgerald Centenary Home Page. This Web site, created and maintained by the University of South Carolina in celebration of the one hundredth anniversary of Fitzgerald's birth, draws from the extensive Matthew J. and Arlyn Bruccoli Collection. It features essays, articles, a biography, and a bibliography, as well as voice and film clips.
(http://www.sc.edu.fitzgerald/index.html)

***American Storytellers*, "F. Scott Fitzgerald's `The Sensible Thing."** In 1998, a film adaptation of Fitzgerald's story "The Sensible Thing,'" written and directed by Elise Robertson, was the premiere episode of the PBS series *American Storytellers*. The series' accompanying Web site, hosted by PBS, features information about the story and its filming, as well as biographies of F. Scott and Zelda Fitzgerald, written by Erika Willett, and a list of primary and secondary readings. (http://www.pbs.org/kteh/amstorytellers)

Video Recordings. Two videos featuring Fitzgerald scholar Matthew J. Bruccoli, *An Introduction to F. Scott Fitzgerald's Fiction* (1988) and *Reading F. Scott Fitzgerald's "The Great Gatsby"* (1988), are available from Omnigraphics of Detroit, Michigan.

JOSEPH ROSENBLUM

Horton Foote

BORN: March 14, 1916, Wharton, Texas
IDENTIFICATION: Mid- to late-twentieth-century American playwright best known for movie scripts and family dramas often set in the small-town South.

Horton Foote achieved success in American theater, film, and television by probing the history of his Texas family and portraying ordinary people with attention to authenticity of character, speech, and setting. His protagonists overcome suffering through the healing power of love. His most popular works are a film adaptation of Harper Lee's novel, *To Kill a Mockingbird* (1962), and his original screenplay, *Tender Mercies* (1983), both of which won Academy Awards, and his play *The Young Man from Atlanta* (1995), which won a Pulitzer Prize.

The Writer's Life

In a rented room in Wharton, Texas, Albert Horton Foote, Jr., was born on March 14, 1916—an event that reconciled his relatives to his parents' marriage. Since 1834, when his great-great-grandfather had come from Alabama, four generations of Hortons had been born in Wharton. The Hortons eventually owned a plantation with 170 slaves but lost it during the post–Civil War Reconstruction years. As Horton Foote grew older, he became fascinated with the stories of his family's disinheritance. He was intrigued by his mother's elopement with his father on Valentine's Day in 1915. Foote's father was considered a wild youth by his relatives, but he later completed a business course and made a modest living as a traveling salesman and shopkeeper. The marriage that many family members denounced lasted for nearly sixty years.

Childhood. During Foote's boyhood, Wharton had about three thousand residents, with nearly as many blacks as whites. The town was bordered on the south by Texas's Colorado River, the periodic flooding of which created tragedies that became fodder for Foote's maturing imagination. He lived with his family in a six-room cottage with a large porch on which his relatives would reminisce about their families' past. He too began telling his own stories, most of which he made up. Foote found that his tales became part of family lore, illustrating both his imaginative powers and his relatives' gullibility.

Schooling. Foote was enrolled in the first grade at the age of five. During these early years he learned as much outside of school as in it. He dug caves and built tree houses. He enjoyed reading—from Rover Boys and Tom Swift stories to Mark Twain's *Tom Sawyer* (1876) and *Huckleberry Finn* (1884).

Foote's childhood idyll ended when his grandfather died in 1925. He never again felt the sheltering security of childhood. He began to wonder about the segregated schools and cemeteries and about his relatives' involvement in the Ku Klux Klan. He learned that the world was complicated by death, racism, and family rivalries.

The Young Actor. When he was eleven, Foote developed a desire to become an actor. His parents hoped in vain that he would grow out of this notion. His determination intensified during high school, when he read the plays of George Bernard Shaw and Noel Coward and acted in plays in his sophomore, junior, and senior years. He developed his

Three-year-old Foote in 1919. Observant and curious, Foote learned much about life from the idle chitchat that took place on his family's front porch.

writing skills by editing the school's yearbook and writing his first story, "A Pinch of Salt," about his family.

In 1932 Foote graduated from high school with the highest average among its boys but refused to go to college, insisting that his parents send him to drama school in New York. His father refused to permit his sixteen-year-old son to "run wild" in Manhattan. After an interval in Dallas, where Foote studied acting, his parents gave him the money to travel to California, where they had relatives. He served a two-year apprenticeship at the Pasadena Playhouse, after which his parents finally allowed him to go to New York City.

Theatrical Career. With pay from menial jobs, Foote supported his studies at the theater school of Tamara Daykarhanova, a distin-

FILMS BASED ON FOOTE'S STORIES

1965 *Baby, the Rain Must Fall*

1966 *The Chase*

1983 *Tender Mercies*

1985 *The Trip to Bountiful*

1986 *On Valentine's Day*

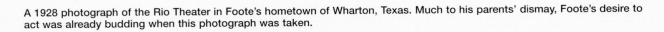

A 1928 photograph of the Rio Theater in Foote's hometown of Wharton, Texas. Much to his parents' dismay, Foote's desire to act was already budding when this photograph was taken.

guished protégée of the Russian director Konstantin Stanislavski, whose "method" technique helped actors use their emotional experiences to develop convincing characterizations. Foote acted in several plays, appeared in a pageant at the 1939 New York World's Fair, and had a leading role in a tour of the patriotic musical *Yankee Doodle Comes to Town.*

With Mary Hunter, a fellow Daykarhanova student, Foote helped found the American Actors Company, a troupe whose goal was to use its actors' regional diversity to develop a distinctly American theater. Drawing on his Texas family for material, Foote wrote such plays as *Texas Town* (1941), *Only the Heart* (1942), and *Out of My House* (1942). During World War II several other Foote plays were produced. For example, Sanford Meisner directed two at his Neighborhood Playhouse, and Martha Graham choreographed another.

In 1944 Foote moved to Washington, D.C., where, with Vincent Donehue, another Daykarhanova colleague, he established a theater workshop. Foote and Donehue shared managing, producing, and directing duties and staged plays by Tennessee Williams and John Millington Synge, as well as four plays by Foote himself. Their successes led them to form Productions, Inc., an independent repertory company. On June 4, 1945, Foote married Lillian Vallish, and the couple had two daughters and two sons.

Writing Work. In 1946 Fred Coe, Donehue's college roommate, became the founding executive producer of the *Philco-Goodyear Playhouse*, a live hour-long dramatic television series. Besides writing plays for Coe, Foote also wrote for the *U.S. Steel Hour, Kraft Playhouse, Gulf Playhouse*, and the *DuPont Show of the Week*. During the 1950s and early 1960s Foote wrote for television while remaining active in the theater. Some of his television scripts were adaptations of his stage plays, and one of his teleplays, *The Trip to Bountiful* (1953), moved with its principal actress, Lillian Gish, to Broadway.

Another actress, Kim Stanley, was discovered by Foote's wife. She appeared in his play *The Chase* (1952), which later became his only novel. Stanley achieved star status on Broadway in the title role of Foote's *The Traveling Lady* (1954). She also headed the cast of his teleplay *Flight* (1956), which Coe produced for the anthology series *Playhouse 90*. Foote also adapted two stories by William Faulkner, *Old Man* (1958) and *Tomorrow* (1960), for this series.

Although Foote had adapted a novel for a United Artists' film, *Storm Fear* (1956), his screenwriting career remained insignificant until his 1962 adaptation of Harper Lee's novel, *To Kill a Mockingbird,* won an Academy

Following in the footsteps of his parents, Foote had a long, happy marriage with Lillian Vallish, his wife of forty-seven years. The two are seen here in a photograph from their personal collection. Her death in 1992 devastated him, and his memories of her inspired him to work again.

HIGHLIGHTS IN FOOTE'S LIFE

1916   Horton Foote is born on March 14 in Wharton, Texas.

1932   Graduates from high school in Wharton.

1933–1935   Studies acting at Pasadena Playhouse in California.

1936–1942   Studies and works as an actor in New York City and on tour.

1941–1944   Writes plays for American Actors Company and Neighborhood Playhouse; moves to Washington, D.C., and teaches acting while writing and directing plays.

1945   Marries Lillian Vallish.

1949   Moves from Washington, D.C., to New York City.

1951–1956   Writes for theater and for such television shows as *Philco-Goodyear Playhouse* and *Playhouse 90*.

1956   Moves from New York City to Nyack, New York; writes first screenplay, *Storm Fear*, and only novel, *The Chase*.

1959   His adaptation of William Faulkner's "Old Man" is nominated for an Emmy Award.

1962   Foote wins an Academy Award and Writers Guild of America Award for his adaptation of Harper Lee's *To Kill a Mockingbird*.

1966   Moves from Nyack to New Hampshire.

1974–1977   Writes several plays in the Orphans' Home cycle.

1978–1979   Returns to New York City; teaches acting; directs three of his plays from the Orphans' Home cycle.

1983   Receives an Academy Award, Writers Guild of American Award, and Christopher Award for his original screenplay *Tender Mercies*.

1985   His screenplay for *The Trip to Bountiful* receives the Independent Film Award and Lumina Award and is nominated for an Academy Award.

1985–1987   Foote begins independent film production of three of the plays in the Orphans' Home cycle.

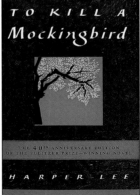

1989   Receives William Inge Lifetime Achievement Award.

1992   Wife, Lillian, dies on August 5 and is buried in Wharton, Texas.

1995   Foote receives Pulitzer Prize for *The Young Man from Atlanta*.

1996   Is inducted into the Theatre Hall of Fame.

1999   Publishes *Farewell: A Memoir of a Texas Childhood*.

2000   Receives a National Medal of Arts from President Bill Clinton.

Award. He wrote the screenplay for *Baby, the Rain Must Fall* (1964), based on his play *The Traveling Lady*. However, producer Sam Spiegel hired Lillian Hellman, not Foote, to write the script for the film based on his novel *The Chase* (1956). Even though Foote's work on the widely criticized Otto Preminger film *Hurry Sundown* (1967) did not appear in the final cut, he shared screenwriting credit with Thomas O. Ryan.

Semiretirement and Back.
After a twenty-five-year career writing for stage, television, and film, Foote virtually vanished from public view for several years. He moved his family to New Hampshire in 1966, unhappy with current trends in theater, motion pictures, and America itself. Catalyzed by his parents' deaths and his wife's encouragement, he wrote several plays in his nine-piece Orphans' Home cycle, which dealt with his family's past and reflected on the breakdown of traditional American values in the 1960s.

Return to Television, Theater, and Films.
In the late 1970s Foote discovered that he still had some passionate supporters, and his plays, long out of fashion, began to be produced. His adaptation of Flannery O'Connor's *The Displaced Person* (1977) appeared on public television. His friend, the actor Robert Duvall, asked for a screenplay, and Foote responded with *Tender Mercies*, which brought Foote his second Academy Award and Duvall his first as an actor.

Foote and his wife left their New Hampshire retreat and settled in New York's Greenwich Village. During the 1980s he began producing the plays of his cycle for stage and film, some of which involved his children as actors and production assistants.

The death of Foote's wife in 1992 reinvigorated his mining of his past, and his plays, both new and old, found fresh audiences. The Signature Theater Company devoted its entire 1994–1995 season to Foote's plays, and in 1995 his *The Young Man From Atlanta* won a Pulitzer Prize. While these works mostly fictionalized his Texas past, his memoir *Farewell: A Memoir of a Texas Childhood* (1999) was a nostalgic re-creation of his early years in Wharton.

President Bill Clinton presents Foote with a National Medal of Arts in Washington, D.C., on December 20, 2000.

The Writer's Work

Playwriting has been the focus of Horton Foote's career. His plays, which often center on personal problems in small-town family life, are meditations on the unavoidable suffering of the human condition and reveal how people can survive and even triumph over such suffering.

Pivotal Concerns in Foote's Work. When asked what the basic themes of his work are, Foote once responded, "acceptance of life" and "preparation for death." Foote's characters live, love, overcome obstacles or are overcome by them, and eventually die. Inextricably intertwined with these life-and-death issues are also the fundamental facts of economic, social, and spiritual life. People need the material necessities that the land provides, but they also need the intangible sense of personal worth and meaning that comes from belonging to a family, community, profession, or even themselves. The changes of time often interfere with the satisfaction of these needs. For example, several of Foote's plays deal with the transition from a traditional southern way of life, with its values of personal and family honor, to a modern capitalist society, with its values of economic and professional success.

Harrison, Texas, Foote's fictional analogue of his home town, is the setting for many of his dramas. The Horton family was important in the region's early history, and though their large plantation vanished after the Civil War, it lived on in Foote's imagination. Consequently, the great themes of southern history—the Civil War, Reconstruction, World War I, and the Great Depression—form the background for his stories of the loneliness of people severed from their roots in traditional society, the depersonalization that accompanies industrialization, and the dehumanization that results when conformity replaces compassion and manipulation replaces love.

Characterization. Most of Foote's major characters battle their ignorance, insecurities, and illusions to make the best of their life situations. Some of his characters courageously accept responsibility for their own lives, whereas others are emotional cripples trapped by greed, grief, or family tragedies. Those characters who break out of their narcissistic cages may grow

This photograph of an early Firestone tire shop in San Marcos, Texas, taken by photographer Russell Lee, reflects an era when small businesses were still thriving. In Foote's plays, corporate growth and development sometimes interfere with one's feelings of personal worth.

into loving people, but others, overwhelmed by life's injustices, may fall into despair. Nevertheless, Foote reveals the humanity in these alienated and abandoned individuals. Broken lives symbolize for him a breakdown in society. Therefore, character development or its dissolution is more important than plot in many of Foote's dramas.

Themes of Attachment and Loss.

Rootlessness suggests a countertheme of attachment, and Foote's psychologically disoriented characters crave connection with others, a place in which to grow, and a sense of identity that will bring them contentment and peace. Some critics describe this theme of attachment as a search for intimacy, a love that brings identity, meaning, and order to life. However, attachment and intimacy are difficult to find and difficult to keep, and when family life is shattered, rootlessness is the result. Foote also realizes that the family itself can become a prison. Ideally the family should satisfy the need to belong and assuage the pains of loss without inhibiting the adventurous and crushing the creative.

Home is more than a physical place for Foote; it can also mean family, religion, work, or whatever roots a person to reality. Similarly, homelessness means more than the loss of a specific place; it is often the loss of emotional and spiritual rootedness and an overwhelming sense of despair. Without ties to place, past, and basic human values, people either act unwisely or fail to act at all. Several of Foote's plays, such as *Tender Mercies*, deal with this struggle with isolation and how healthy attachment helps to save the rootless.

Foote and Film.

During the 1960s Foote became a successful Hollywood screenwriter, and despite his extensive work in theater and television, he is best known for such film scripts as *To Kill a Mockingbird*, *Tender Mercies*, and *The Trip to Bountiful*. He enjoyed bringing these works to the screen but was unhappy with his collaboration on other Hollywood projects. Although he was a consultant on *The Chase* (1966), which was based on his novel, the film suffered because of the conflicts among the producer Sam Spiegel, who wanted total control, the director Arthur Penn, who lost artistic control, and the screenwriter Lillian Hellman, who felt her script had been subverted. Foote, whose novel had disappeared into the film, had no fondness for what he saw on the screen.

Although Foote got along well with Otto Preminger, the director of *Hurry Sundown*, the two men disagreed about how the film should be done, and not a word of Foote's remained in the final script. Nevertheless, as a favor to Preminger, and because he needed the money, he agreed to share screen credit with the writer whose words

Thomas Hart Benton's 1931 watercolor pen-and-ink drawing, entitled *Western Tourist Camp*, depicts slumbered figures who, for whatever reason, are away from home. The slouched individuals imply crushed spirits and reflect Foote's strong theme of emotional and spiritual rootlessness due to detachment from one's home—or from whatever makes one feel like they are home.

PLAYS

1940	The Wharton Dance
1941	Texas Town
1942	Out of My House
1942	Only the Heart
1943	Two Southern Idylls: Miss Lou and The Girls
1944	The Lonely
1944	Goodbye to Richmond
1944	Homecoming
1944	In My Beginning
1944	People in the Show
1944	Return
1948	Celebration
1952	The Chase
1953	The Trip to Bountiful
1954	The Traveling Lady
1961	Night of the Storm (later retitled Roots in a Parched Land)
1963	Tomorrow
1971	Gone with the Wind
1976	A Young Lady of Property
1977	Night Seasons
1979	1918
1980	In a Coffin in Egypt
1980	Valentine's Day
1981	The Man Who Climbed Pecan Trees
1982	The Old Friends
1982	The Roads to Home (a trilogy: Nightingale, The Dearest of Friends, and Spring Dance)
1983	Cousins
1984	Courtship
1985	The One-Armed Man
1985	The Prisoner's Song
1986	The Widow Claire
1986	Lily Dale
1988	The Habitation of Dragons
1989	Dividing the Estate
1989	The Death of Papa
1990	Talking Pictures
1993	Night Seasons
1995	God's Pictures
1995	Laura Dennis
1995	Young Man from Atlanta

SCREENPLAYS

1956	Storm Fear
1962	To Kill a Mockingbird
1964	Baby, the Rain Must Fall
1967	Hurry Sundown (with Thomas O. Ryan)
1968	The Stalking Moon
1971	Tomorrow
1983	Tender Mercies
1984	1918
1985	On Valentine's Day
1985	The Trip to Bountiful
1986	Courtship
1991	Convicts
1992	Of Mice and Men
1993	Pastor's Son
1994	The Man of the House
1996	Lily Dale

TELEVISION PLAYS

1947	Only the Heart
1951	Ludie Brooks
1952	The Travelers
1953	The Trip to Bountiful
1953	Rocking Chair
1955	Roads to Home
1956	Flight
1956	Drugstore: Sunday Noon
1957	Member of the Family
1959	Old Man
1960	The Shape of the River
1960	The Night of the Storm (also known as Roots in a Parched Ground)
1960	Tomorrow
1964	The Gambling Heart
1977	The Displaced Person
1980	Barn Burning
1987	The Story of a Marriage
1992	The Habitation of Dragons

LONG FICTION

1956	The Chase

NONFICTION

1989	From Uncertain to Blue (with Keith Carter)
1999	Farewell: A Memoir of a Texas Childhood

ROOTS IN A PARCHED GROUND
CONVICTS
LILY DALE
THE WIDOW CLAIRE
4 PLAYS FROM THE ORPHANS' HOME CYCLE
HORTON FOOTE

were used. Disillusioned with some of his Hollywood experiences, he found fulfillment in writing *Tender Mercies* for Robert Duvall. Many critics consider this script to be Foote's finest. Through it, both he and his chief character were able to overcome suffering to realize the importance of honesty, decency, and compassion.

Foote's Legacy. Throughout his long career Foote has had both popular and critical successes and failures. Some critics have called him America's greatest playwright. Katherine Anne Porter, a fellow Texas writer, acclaimed him as a "national treasure." This praise must be balanced by the evaluations of other critics, who situate Foote's work in the center—rather than near the top—of the hierarchy of America's dramatists. Still others place Foote near the bottom, believing his themes unoriginal, his techniques out of date, and his plays plotless and sentimental.

Foote's work has passed in and out of fashion and has been both forgotten and revived. Undeterred by the vagaries of fashion and his own fortunes, he maintained his spare style and his focus on the lives of ordinary Americans. One of his greatest strengths as a writer is the authenticity of his characters, their speech, and the world they inhabit. In choosing to investigate such ordinary people and to give them the attention they deserve, he captures the diversity of the American people and their various comic and tragic stories. Although he is sometimes seen as a regional writer, he knows the people of Texas so deeply that he also knows the rest of the United States and indeed the entire world.

BIBLIOGRAPHY

Briley, Rebecca L. *You Can Go Home Again: The Focus on Family in the Works of Horton Foote*. New York: Peter Lang, 1994.

Bossler, Gregory. "Horton Foote: The Bard of Wharton." *The Dramatist Magazine* 2 (September/October 1999): 4–11.

Burckhardt, Marian. "Horton Foote's Many Roads Home." *Commonweal* 115 (February 26, 1988): 110–115.

Cincotti, Joseph A. "Horton Foote: The Trip from Wharton." In *Backstory 3: Interviews with Screenwriters of the 1960s*, edited by Patrick McGilligan. Berkeley: University of California Press, 1997.

Davis, Ronald L. "Roots in Parched Ground: An Interview with Horton Foote." *Southwest Review* 73 (Summer 1988): 298–318.

Engel, Joel, ed. *Screenwriters on Screenwriting*. New York: Hyperion Press, 1995.

Wood, Gerald C. *Horton Foote and the Theater of Intimacy*. Baton Rouge: Louisiana State University Press, 1998.

———, Wood, Gerald C. and Kimball King, eds. *Horton Foote: A Casebook*. New York: Garland, 1997.

Wright, Timothy. "A Conversation with Horton Foote." *Image: A Journal of the Arts and Religion* 20 (Summer 1998): 45–57.

SOME INSPIRATIONS BEHIND FOOTE'S WORK

Since a particular place and its people have inspired so much of his work, Horton Foote has often been interviewed about them. His reply has been that he did not choose Wharton, Texas, or his family; they chose him. From the start he realized that Gulf coast Texas would be his fictional home, just as the mythical Yoknapatawpha County of Mississippi was William Faulkner's.

Foote was also inspired by such southern writers as Flannery O'Connor and Eudora Welty, whose works have a strong sense of place: O'Connor's in Georgia and Welty's in Jackson, Mississippi. Foote's extensive reading of classic playwrights, such as Henrik Ibsen, August Strindberg, and Anton Chekhov as well as the American dramatists Eugene O'Neill and Tennessee Williams, was also influential. Like Chekhov, Foote has explored the fading of traditional life and values in the modern world. Like O'Neill, he has also created characters who are homeless wanderers in a soulless universe. However, Foote's characters, unlike O'Neill's, sometimes heal their existential wounds through connection to the world's enduring values. Foote's own family helped him to develop the compassion that he hopes, through his plays, will help to heal a wounded humanity.

TENDER MERCIES

Genre: Screenplay
Subgenre: Romantic drama
Produced: 1983
Time period: 1970s
Setting: Small Texas town

Themes and Issues. Horton Foote took the title of this screenplay from a phrase that appears frequently in the Bible's Book of Psalms. In that book, the sick, sinners, and troubled rely on the "tender mercies" of God to bring them health, forgiveness, and peace. The central issue of the film is whether love can change the life of a down-and-out alcoholic. The healing power of love is a theme in much of Foote's work, but how that healing takes place is often at issue. Love must be freely given, but its acceptance determines its efficacy. Foote's characters cooperate in their own healing just as his victims participate in their own destruction. To be healed and redeemed, the alcoholic singer Mac Sledge must learn to see himself anew. A person's identity is not discovered apart from others; Mac can achieve self-redemption only by recognizing his connection to both his old and new families.

The Plot. Mac Sledge, drunk and out of money, passes out at a rural Texas motel. The next morning, he meets its owner, Rosa Lee, a young widow who will allow him to work for his room and board if he agrees to stop drinking. He begins to rebuild his life and forms a warm relationship with Rosa Lee and her young son, whose father was killed in the Vietnam War. Mac and Rosa eventually marry.

A reporter's visit reveals that Mac Sledge had formerly been a successful country-western singer and that he has a teenage daughter, Sue Anne, by his ex-wife, the country-western singer Dixie Scott. After the local paper prints a story about Mac, members of a local band visit him for inspiration and advice, and he begins writing music again. When Dixie gives a concert in Austin, Mac wants to see his daughter, but Dixie tries to keep her away from him.

Despite these obstacles, Sue Anne visits Mac, and they are reconciled. She is a rebel who is having an affair with one of her mother's musicians. Sue Anne elopes with him and is killed in a car crash. Mac's depression lightens when he returns from her funeral with a gift of a football for his stepson. Rosa Lee watches Mac and her son playing in the field opposite her motel and realizes that her new family is truly beginning to unite.

Analysis. The film's subject is not only Mac's recovery from alcoholism but also his coming to terms with his failed career and marriage. Like many of Foote's characters, Mac Sledge is haunted by a sense of disjointedness. Few

William Gropper's 1932 oil painting *Migration* (Arizona State University Museum of Art, Tucson, Arizona) renders a family fleeing their failing farm during the Dust Bowl era. The journey of the underdog is also evident in Foote's 1983 screenplay, *Tender Mercies*, the story of a down-and-out alcoholic figuratively finding his way home with the help of his new wife and son.

critics see Foote as a primarily religious writer, but his characters often express a genuine hunger for spiritual direction and meaning. Foote treats Rosa Lee's religion as authentic, and when Mac is baptized in her church, his repentance and reconciliation are given religious validation.

Critics were widely divided over the success and significance of *Tender Mercies*. Those who were unhappy with the film found its lack of action "wearisome," its cinematography constricted, and its writing plain. the *New Yorker* film critic Pauline Kael bluntly stated that *Tender Mercies* proved that "a movie doesn't have to be long to be ponderous." In contrast, those who praised the film called Foote's screenplay his crowning achievement. Others proclaimed it a classic and declared that it was the most honest film depiction of small-town life in the Bible Belt. Those who thought highly of the film admired its refreshingly life-affirming qualities, which went against the cynicism then fashionable in Hollywood.

SOURCES FOR FURTHER STUDY

Cincotti, Joseph A. "Horton Foote: The Trip from Wharton." In *Backstory 3: Interviews with Screenwriters of the 1960s*, edited by Patrick McGilligan. Berkeley: University of California Press, 1997.

Kael, Pauline. *For Keeps*. New York: Dutton, 1994.

Ozer, Jerome S., ed. "Tender Mercies." *Film Review Annual*. Englewood, N.J.: Jerome S. Ozer, 1984.

TO KILL A MOCKINGBIRD

    Genre: Screenplay
    Subgenre: Bildungsroman
    Produced: 1962
    Time period: Early 1930s
    Setting: Small Alabama town

Themes and Issues: Since Foote had dealt with the issues of generational conflict and southern racism in several of his own works, he was a natural choice to adapt Harper Lee's novel, *To Kill a Mockingbird* (1960), for the screen. Like Lee's, Foote's fictional children want to explore their world, but they need deeply rooted values to do so. Foote portrays the adults in the story as troubled by racism, and he uses his experience of his own family's racist past to deal sensitively with the problems facing Lee's African American characters. In narrating the story as a bildungsroman from a child's viewpoint, expressing Scout's coming-of-age, Foote both simplifies and deepens his themes. The children want perplexing issues resolved in clear-cut categories of good and evil, while the adults understand the often complex and irrational desires of the human heart.

The Plot. Atticus Finch, a sensitive and idealistic lawyer, is a widower with two adventurous children: six-year-old Scout and her

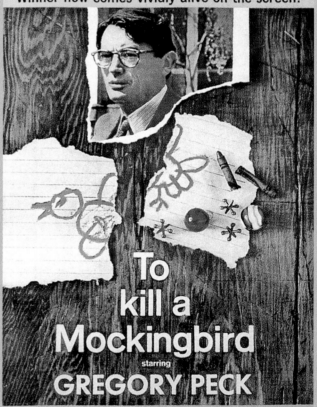

A poster promoting the 1962 motion picture adaptation of Harper Lee's classic novel, *To Kill a Mockingbird*, one of the two screenplays for which Foote took home Academy Awards. Gregory Peck was honored with the Academy Award for Best Actor for his portrayal of Atticus Finch, the dedicated lawyer and loving father in *To Kill a Mockingbird*.

ten-year-old brother, Jem. The story, told in retrospect by a much older Scout, begins in a summer during the Great Depression of the 1930s. The children, who amuse themselves by rolling each other in a tire, are intrigued by a mysterious man who lives in an old house in their neighborhood. Their young imaginations mythologize the unseen Boo Radley as a madman with such fearsome powers that his father has had to chain him to a bed. They enjoy telling fantastic Boo stories to Dill, a summertime visitor who is gullible, small, and eccentric. (Harper Lee modeled Dill on her childhood friend Truman Capote.)

As distorted as the children's view of Boo Radley is, most townspeople distort the actions of Tom Robinson, an African American, even more and with much more dangerous consequences. Robinson is accused of raping Mayella Ewell, a poor white girl, and Atticus Finch, convinced of Robinson's innocence, agrees to defend him. However, most of the white townspeople, who believe that Robinson is guilty, make threats against Atticus, his client, and his children. When a lynch mob gathers outside the jail, Atticus stands guard between his client and the mob, but it is Scout who defuses the threat. Although she is at the scene in disobedience to her father's command, she calmly talks to the mob members about their children—her friends and classmates. This calms their rage, and they disperse.

During Robinson's trial, which Scout and Jem watch with the African American community from the courthouse's upper gallery, Atticus Finch ably and eloquently demonstrates his client's innocence. Mayella Ewell actually made sexual advances to Robinson, which he rebuffed, and Mayella's father beat her for her behavior. Despite Finch's convincing arguments, the all-white jury convicts Robinson, who is later shot to death in an alleged escape attempt.

After the trial Scout escapes being killed by Mayella's father when Boo Radley, who had been secretly watching over Scout and Jem, kills their attacker. Though Boo Radley is the town simpleton, he nevertheless understands evil. In the final scene, Scout, who now sees Boo as her savior, walks him home, with a new understanding of how children and adults can learn from each other.

Analysis. *To Kill a Mockingbird* was successful with both audiences and Academy Award voters. Those critics who praised the film viewed its childhood and adult story lines as individually and interactively successful. They admired the spirit and charm of the children's adventures and also found Finch's doomed defense of Tom Robinson relevant to an America still struggling to come to terms with its racially troubled past and present. Other critics, in contrast, argued that the two stories never really became meaningfully entwined, suggesting that the children's story romanticized youthful innocence and that the corruption of the adults was exaggerated. Furthermore, Foote's critics found his account of race relations paternalistic, self-righteous, and filled with phony liberalism.

Over time, more sophisticated analyses appeared. For example, some now see the film as part of a series, along with such precursors as William Faulkner and Ben Maddows's *Intruder in the Dust* (1949) and Willis Goldbeck and James Warner Bellah's *Sergeant Rutledge* (1960), in which the Hollywood stereotype of the servile African American was replaced by a characterization emphasizing black nobility and dignity. Foote's treatment of Atticus and his children has also found admirers who appreciate his insightful portrayal of the parent-child relationship and his skillful communication of the critical steps that a child follows on the way to emotional and intellectual maturity.

SOURCES FOR FURTHER STUDY

Belton, John. *Cinema Stylists.* Lanham, Md.: Scarecrow Press, 1983.

Campbell, Virginia. "To Kill a Mockingbird." In *Magill's Survey of Cinema: English Language Films, First Series*, edited by Frank N. Magill. Vol. 4. Englewood Cliffs, N.J.: Salem Press, 1980.

Crowther, Bosley. "To Kill a Mockingbird." In *The New York Times Film Reviews, 1959–1968*. Vol. 5. New York: New York Times and Arno Press, 1970.

Kael, Pauline. *5001 Nights at the Movies: A Guide from A to Z*. New York: Holt, Rinehart and Winston, 1982.

THE YOUNG MAN FROM ATLANTA

Genre: Play
Subgenre: Family drama
Produced: 1995
Time period: Spring 1950
Setting: Houston, Texas

Themes and Issues. Foote's only play to win a Pulitzer Prize, *The Young Man from Atlanta*, examines the issues of family, grief, and self-delusion. As do several of Foote's previous works, this play centers on a family's loss of wealth, security, and love. Foote's thematic focus is on the fragility of family happiness, as menacing secrets are buried like time bombs beneath a seemingly tranquil facade. A son's suicide casts into doubt all that his parents hold dear.

Foote also raises the issues of religion and homosexuality: religion provides solace for the mother's grief, while the possibility of her son's homosexuality is the secret that she cannot even verbalize. However, as several critics pointed out, Foote's work is not a "gay play," in that no character refers even euphemistically to the truth of the relationship between the couple's son and the young man from Atlanta. Most intriguing is Foote's decision to keep his deepest meanings ambiguous by forcing his principal characters to decide whether the words of this young man—who is never seen by the audience—are true.

The Plot. Before the play begins, its central event has already occurred: the drowning

The actor Rip Torn (right) played the role of Will Kidder in the 1997 New York production of Foote's Pulitzer Prize–winning play, *The Young Man from Atlanta*. Here, Will shows his coworker Tom, played by actor Marcus Giamatti, a photograph of his deceased son, Bill. The mystery that surrounds Bill's death and the questions that arise about his roommate's character form the compelling components of Foote's play.

death of Bill, the thirty-seven-year-old bachelor son of Will and Lily Dale Kidder. Will Kidder, the sixty-four-year-old chief executive of a wholesale grocery company, has just bought a $200,000 home. A self-made man, he wants the best of everything but is being forced to confront the worst. He discovers he has heart disease, his son has died in what he suspects was a suicide, and the company's owner has fired him.

Lily, Will's submissive wife, has heard rumors about her son's suicide but refuses to believe them. Instead, she believes Randy Carter, Bill's roommate from Atlanta, who reassures her of the religiosity of her son. Thankful for Randy's consoling words, she takes pity on him when he tells her of his family's many problems. She gives him large sums of money despite her husband's protests. Eventually the audience learns about a number of Bills, each one the construct of a particular character.

Similarly, Randy himself is a puzzle. Is he a parasite who lived off Bill financially and emotionally or is he a victim of his family's troubles? Since Randy Carter is never seen, it is difficult to determine whether the real Randy is Bill's Randy, Will's Randy, or Lily's Randy. In the end, the young man from Atlanta makes Will and Lily realize how much they need each other, even though the illusions they embrace differ dramatically.

Analysis. The characters of Will and Lily Kidder appeared in earlier Foote plays, and this play can be seen as the tenth in his nine-play Orphans' Home cycle. With its elegiac tone, Foote seems finally to be saying farewell to these characters. As in his other plays, his men and women are confronted with disruptive changes. They recognize that beliefs about reality are often determined by desire. Foote was amused by the way that various audience members came to contradictory conclusions about his own and his principal characters' truthfulness.

Critics who disliked the play pointed to its uninspired depiction of American society and its pedestrian dialogue. One critic was surprised that Foote, at eighty, could continue to get his plays produced. Another wondered how many times Foote could write the same boring, old-fashioned, sentimental play. The play's admirers praised Foote's handling of the son's death and suggested that the parents' response revealed the pros and cons of the American Dream. It is good that optimism allows people to overcome debilitating difficulties, but it is bad when this optimism blinds people to basic truths that need to be faced rather than fantasized away.

SOURCES FOR FURTHER STUDY

Canby, Vincent. "Nameless Menace in Latest by Foote." *New York Times*, January 30, 1995, 13, 16.

Feingold, Michael. "The Normal Foote." *Village Voice*, February 7, 1995, 81.

Simon, John. "With Blunt Tools." *New York Magazine* 28 (February 27, 1995): 115–117.

Other Works

THE ORPHANS' HOME CYCLE (1961–1989). This series of nine interrelated plays, written mostly in the 1970s and 1980s, begins with *Night of the Storm* (later retitled *Roots in a Parched Land*) and ends with *The Death of Papa*. The series is based on Foote's own family history, and its hero is Horace Robedaux, who is modeled on Foote's grandfather. Much of the action is set in the fictional town of Harrison, Texas. The cycle covers the years from 1902, when Horace Robedaux's father dies, to 1928, when Elizabeth Robedaux's father dies.

Courtship (1984), a pivotal play in the cycle, deals with how Horace Robedaux came to marry Elizabeth Vaughn. Earlier plays treat Horace's adventures after he leaves home as a twelve-year-old following the death of his father. Other plays chronicle events in the history of the Robedaux and Vaughn families during World War I, the influenza epidemic of 1918, and the economic ups and downs of the 1920s.

Despite Elizabeth Robedaux's wish in *Valentine's Day* that everything in her life stay the same, she realizes that permanence is one thing that life will never give her. Reflecting the families' changing fortunes is the decline of Harrison's plantation aristocracy and the rise of its capitalist class. In the last play, *The Death of Papa* (1989), Foote shows how one day can change an entire family. Based on Foote's recollections of his grandfather's death, the play embodies his own loss of emotional security.

According to Foote, his cycle is a glorification of the human spirit's ability to carry on despite suffering and death. He has said that he wrote these plays to help himself "separate what is permanent from what is not." For such critics as John Simon, Foote's cycle is "an unmitigated bore, as only something based on a group of plays about one's own nice, dull family by a nice, sentimentalizing playwright can be." Others see the cycle as a significant family epic, guaranteeing Foote "a deservedly permanent place in American theater."

THE TRIP TO BOUNTIFUL (1985). This film's screenplay, nominated for an Academy Award, grew out of a teleplay that Foote ex-panded into a three-act stage version in 1953. The story centers on Carrie Watts, an old widow living unhappily in a cramped Houston apartment with her son and daughter-in-law. She has one last wish—to return to Bountiful, the small Texas town where she was born and grew up. She surreptitiously leaves Houston and on the bus meets a soldier's wife with whom she exchanges memories. When her bus arrives at the town nearest Bountiful, she learns from the sheriff that her son is coming to get her, that her last friend in the area has died, and that Bountiful is essentially a ghost town. Nevertheless, the sheriff takes Carrie to the dead town, which for her is alive with memories. When her son and his wife arrive, Carrie tries to draw them into her remembrances, but they resist. She wants to relive the past, but they want to forget it.

Like many of Foote's other works, *The Trip to Bountiful* is about going home. Twenty years of urban life have corroded Carrie's spirit. Bountiful symbolizes an idyllic rural past, when Carrie was young, beautiful, and full of hope. However, her trip forces her to accept the inevitability of change and to make peace with her present family. It also raises questions about the spiritual health of modern society and how people contentedly caged in the present can be freed by the past to accept its deeper set of values.

Resources

The major collection of Horton Foote manuscripts is at the Degolyer Library at Southern Methodist University in Dallas, Texas. The Horton Foote Collection contains many boxes of materials from Foote's life and career, including grade school report cards, photographs, and correspondence. The collection also has original drafts, manuscripts, and typescripts of his plays. Other sources of interest to students of Horton Foote include the following:

Wharton County Historical Museum. In Wharton, Foote's hometown, there is a museum that contains a biographical file on the playwright, but it will also house copies of all of the papers in the Horton Foote Collection at Southern Methodist University.

Harry Ransom Research Humanities Center. This center is located at the University of Texas at Austin. The Tennessee Williams Collection features correspondence between Foote and Williams.

ROBERT J. PARADOWSKI

Robert Frost

BORN: March 26, 1874, San Francisco, California
DIED: January 29, 1963, Boston, Massachusetts
IDENTIFICATION: Modern American poet known for his lyric and dramatic nature poems set in a New England landscape.

Although Robert Frost wrote a good deal of his work in the modernist period, he defined himself and his work largely in opposition to the high literary modernism of Ezra Pound and T. S. Eliot. A pastoralist by temperament and inclination, Frost renewed the vernacular tradition in American poetry. He observed and recorded little-noticed details of the natural landscape, professing the "sound of sense" and finding significance in words and tones. His rich, complex, and allusive poems are accessible to the ordinary reader. He was a self-professed "poet for all sorts and kinds," who became a literary celebrity by the end of his life. He won an unprecedented four Pulitzer Prizes and re-cited "The Gift Outright" at President John F. Kennedy's inauguration in 1961, by which time he had become a national symbol. Frost has remained one of the most popular and preeminent twentieth-century American poets.

The Writer's Life

Robert Lee Frost was born on March 26, 1874, in a small apartment on Washington Street in San Francisco, California. He was the elder of two children born to William Prescott Frost, Jr., and Isabelle Moodie Frost, called Belle.

Frost's father was a mercurial and consumptive journalist and would-be Democratic politician with pro-southern sympathies who, after graduating from Harvard University in 1872, left New England to try his luck in the West. He met his future wife while both of them taught at Lewistown Academy in Pennsylvania. The couple married in 1873 and settled in San Francisco, where Will Frost worked as a newspaperman and editor for a decade until his death from tuberculosis in 1885.

Childhood. Will Frost's rash and impulsive behavior created an unstable family environment. The politically ambitious but improvident Will was mismatched with his mystical, Scottish-born wife, Belle, who increasingly turned for solace to the teachings of the eighteenth-century Swedish theologian Emanuel Swedenborg after her husband began drinking heavily. Young Frost accompanied his father on long walks through San Francisco, visiting bars and Democratic political rallies. He was tutored at home by his mother, who introduced him to poetry and inspirational literature and sheltered him from Will's abuse.

Will's premature death left his family nearly destitute, and Belle reluctantly decided to return east in 1885 with her two young children to live with her retired in-laws in the mill town of Lawrence, Massachusetts. Frost spent his teenage years in Lawrence, while his mother taught at various local elementary schools. Belle Frost never remarried but instead devoted herself to her children, especially to her son, who showed an early interest in poetry. The family lived modestly on Belle's teacher's salary, and Frost worked summers and held part-time jobs to help his family. His younger sister, Jeanie, showed early signs of the mental instability that would shadow her adult life. Throughout high school, Frost was an excellent student, a good athlete, a debater, and editor of his high school newspaper. In 1892, he graduated as covaledictorian with Elinor Miriam White, whom he would marry three years later.

This undated photograph of Frost as an infant was taken in San Francisco, where his family lived until 1885.

College Years. Discouraged by his grandparents from applying to Harvard

University, Frost entered Dartmouth College in the fall of 1892 but left after one semester, dissatisfied with college life. More than anything else, he missed Elinor, who had enrolled in St. Lawrence University in Canton, New York. They had become secretly engaged the previous summer, and Frost was eager to marry, despite their youth. He was determined to become a poet and was willing to do odd jobs to support himself. With the money from the sale of his first poem "My Butterfly," in 1894, he published two copies of a small gift book, *Twilight*, as a present for Elinor. Her indifference to the book led Frost to make an impulsive trip south to the Great Dismal Swamp in Virginia and North Carolina, from which he was rescued by a group of genial hunters. The couple finally married on December 19, 1895.

Husband, Poet, and Farmer.

The young couple began their marriage in cramped quarters, living with Frost's mother. After another year of teaching, Frost applied to Harvard as a special student and was admitted in the fall of 1897. He studied Greek and Latin for three semesters, distinguishing himself academically but nevertheless withdrawing by March 1899 to return to Lawrence.

That spring, Frost, prone to tuberculosis, was persuaded to move to the country to improve his health. The family moved to a small farm in Derry, New Hampshire, where Frost began to raise chickens and write poetry during the evenings, supported by a small annuity from his grandfather. Many of Frost's most famous pastoral poems and much of his first three volumes were written during these Derry years, although most were not published until

after 1912. By 1905, his family had grown to include three daughters and a son; two other children were lost in infancy. After discovering that his style of casual farming would not pay, Frost began to teach at Pinkerton Academy, a small private school in Derry, where he remained until 1911. His reputation as an innovative teacher led to an appointment at the New Hampshire Normal School, the state teacher's college, in Plymouth, where he remained for one year. Dissatisfied with the restrictions of teaching and still hoping to become a recognized poet, Robert and Elinor decided to sell the Derry farm and move to

Frost with his wife, Elinor, and their four children: Lesley and Irma, the older girls; Marjorie, the youngest child; and Carol, the only surviving boy. This photograph was taken in Bridgewater, New Hampshire, in 1915, after the Frosts returned from a three-year stay in Europe.

England in the autumn of 1912. Frost hoped to find a British publisher and gain recognition among English critics.

England. The three years that Frost spent in England, from 1912 to 1915, proved to be the most momentous of his career. He found a London publisher for his first two poetry volumes, *A Boy's Will* (1913) and *North of Boston* (1914), and made important literary contacts, among them Ezra Pound, who introduced Frost to the London literary circles, where he quickly made friends among the Georgian poets. His strongest and most significant friendship, however, was with the Welsh-born poet Edward Thomas, with whom Frost shared a common temperament and interest in pastoral poetry.

The Return to America. With the outbreak of World War I in 1914, Frost and his family decided to return to the United States, arriving in 1915. The favorable reviews of Frost's first two poetry volumes had generated considerable interest in his work, and he quickly found an American publisher in Henry Holt. The Frosts purchased a farm in Franconia, New Hampshire, and Frost began a series of literary tours and public readings. An invitation from Amherst College president Alexander Micklejohn led to Frost's accepting a newly created position as poet-in-residence at Amherst in 1916. Frost became the first American poet to serve as a creative writer-in-residence, a post that largely freed him from regular teaching responsibilities, although he did teach an occasional seminar and gave regular public readings. He would spend much of the rest of his career affiliated with Amherst, as well as the University of Michigan, Harvard, and Dartmouth, in a series of special appointments and honorary professorships.

Growing Recognition. Beginning in the 1920s, Frost's literary reputation grew steadily, earning him four Pulitzer Prizes, in the years 1924, 1931, 1937, and 1943. For the rest of his career, Frost published poetry volumes on a regular basis. A selected edition of his poems appeared in 1923, followed by a collected edi-

tion in 1930. Through the favorable reviews of friends such as the critics Louis Untermeyer and Bernard DeVoto, Frost became a significant alternative voice to the literary modernism of Ezra Pound and T. S. Eliot. During the depression years of the 1930s, however, Frost's social and political conservatism opened him to attacks from leftist critics.

Family Tragedies. Frost was restless and single-minded in his pursuit of a literary career, moving several times between Amherst and the University of Michigan, sometimes at a hardship to his family. Frost enjoyed "barding about" and went on long public lecture tours each year, while Elinor missed the stability of their years in Derry and preferred the quiet of home. The Frosts were a close family; they educated their four children at home and spent much time outdoors with them during their early years. Frost and his wife were somewhat overprotective of their four children, who nevertheless experienced more than their share of misfortune. Their four-year-old son Elliott died of cholera in 1900; in 1934, their youngest daughter, Marjorie, died from complications of childbirth; their son Carol suffered from depression and committed suicide in 1940; and their daughter Irma was mentally unstable. Frost was estranged from his eldest daughter, Lesley, until late in his life.

Always emotionally insecure, Frost came to suspect that Elinor may have resented the life they shared. She had a history of congenital heart disease, which was complicated by eight pregnancies and an operation for breast cancer. She suffered a serious heart attack in Florida in the winter of 1938, lapsed into unconsciousness, and died two days later. Frost was despondent and blamed himself for her death. He became emotionally unstable for several years afterward until he found a surrogate family relationship with Ted and Kay Morrison, a young Harvard faculty couple whom he had met several years earlier at the Bread Loaf Writers' Conference in Middlebury, Vermont. Kay Morrison became Frost's personal secretary and the object of his attention.

In this delightful photograph, taken in 1945, Frost sits on the floor of a cabin in Ripton, Vermont, intent on the actions of his granddaughter. She is about to release the long narrow sticks called jackstraws. The purpose of the game jackstraws (sometimes called pick-up-sticks) is to pick up, one at a time, as many sticks as possible without disturbing the remaining sticks. Frost's granddaughters, Elinor and Lesley Lee Francis, have their backs to the camera. His oldest daughter, Lesley, with whom he had become reconciled after a long estrangement, sits beside him.

The Later Years. Frost remained physically and mentally active well beyond middle age, and he continued his public appearances up until the end of his life. He gradually became a more prominent public figure, assuming the persona of the sagacious Yankee poet-farmer. Frost enjoyed a renewed period of creativity during the last two decades of his life, appearing on television talk shows and serving as the poetry consultant to the Library of Congress in 1958. Both his seventy-fifth and eighty-fifth birthdays were celebrated with honorary dinners. At the latter, in 1959, the influential critic Lionel Trilling gave a famous speech in which he called Frost "a terrifying poet."

Frost traveled for the U.S. State Department to Brazil in 1954 and later to Israel and Greece in 1961. He was awarded honorary doctorates by Oxford and Cambridge Universities in 1957, becoming the only American poet besides Henry Wadsworth Longfellow and Robert Lowell to be so honored. Frost recited "The Gift Outright" at President John F. Kennedy's inauguration on January 20, 1961. A year later he was invited by Kennedy to travel to the Soviet Union as part of a cultural exchange program, at which time he met Premier Nikita Khrushchev at the Black Sea resort of Gagra. Arriving home ill and exhausted, Frost misrepresented a remark by Khrushchev, that Americans were allegedly "too liberal to fight," which heightened Cold War tensions and strained Frost's friendship with Kennedy.

In December 1962 Frost underwent an operation for prostate and bladder cancer and suffered a pulmonary embolism. In January 1963, while he was still in the hospital, he was awarded the Bollingen Prize for Poetry. He suffered another pulmonary embolism and died in Boston, Massachusetts, on January 29. A public service was held at Johnson Chapel at Amherst College on February 17, and the poet's ashes were interred in his family plot in Old Bennington, Vermont, on June 16.

HIGHLIGHTS IN FROST'S LIFE

1874   Robert Lee Frost is born on March 26 in San Francisco, California.

1885   Father, William Prescott Frost, dies of tuberculosis; Frost moves to Lawrence, Massachusetts, with mother and sister.

1892   Graduates as covaledictorian from Lawrence High School; studies for a semester at Dartmouth College in New Hampshire.

1894   Publishes first poem, "My Butterfly," in *The Independent*.

1895   Marries Elinor White in Lawrence, Massachusetts.

1896   Son Elliott is born.

1897   Frost enters Harvard University as a special student.

1899   Withdraws from Harvard after three semesters; daughter Lesley is born; Frost takes up poultry farming in New Hampshire.

1900   Son Elliott dies of cholera; family moves to thirty-acre farm in Derry, New Hampshire; Frost's mother dies of cancer.

1902   Son Carol is born.

1903   Daughter Irma is born.

1905   Daughter Marjorie is born.

1906   Frost begins teaching at Pinkerton Academy in Derry, New Hampshire.

1911   Accepts offer to teach at the State Normal School in Plymouth, New Hampshire; sells the Derry farm.

1912   Resigns from teaching position and moves family to England to devote himself to writing.

1913   Publishes first poetry volume, *A Boy's Will*, in London; meets Ezra Pound and other imagist and Georgian poets; forms close friendship with Edward Thomas.

1914   Publishes second poetry volume, *North of Boston*; moves to Gloucestershire.

1915   Returns with his family to New York; publishes first two poetry volumes in the United States with Henry Holt and Company; moves to a farm in Franconia, New Hampshire.

1916   Begins teaching at Amherst College in Amherst, Massachusetts; publishes third poetry volume, *Mountain Interval*.

1921   Begins teaching summers at the Bread Loaf Writers' Conference in Middlebury, Vermont; accepts fellowship at the University of Michigan.

1924 Is awarded first Pulitzer Prize, for *New Hampshire: A Poem with Notes and Grace Notes* (1923).

1926 Rejoins Amherst College as a part-time professor of English.

1930 Is elected to American Academy of Arts and Letters.

1931 Is awarded second Pulitzer Prize, for *Collected Poems*.

1934 Daughter Marjorie dies in childbirth.

1936 Frost begins appointment as Charles Eliot Norton Professor of Poetry at Harvard University.

1937 Is awarded third Pulitzer Prize, for *A Further Range* (1936).

1938 Wife Elinor dies of heart failure in Gainesville, Florida.

1939 Frost accepts appointment as Ralph Waldo Emerson Fellow in Poetry at Harvard.

1940 Son Carol commits suicide.

1941 Frost moves to Cambridge, Massachusetts; accepts appointment as Fellow in American Civilization at Harvard.

1943 Is awarded fourth Pulitzer Prize, for *A Witness Tree* (1942).

1945 Accepts appointment as Ticknor Fellow at Dartmouth College.

1949 Returns to Amherst College as Simpson Lecturer in Literature.

1950 Is honored by U.S. Senate on his seventy-fifth birthday.

1954 Travels to Brazil with his daughter Lesley.

1957 Is awarded honorary doctorates by Oxford and Cambridge Universities.

1959 Lionel Trilling speaks at Frost's eighty-fifth birthday dinner.

1961 Frost recites "The Gift Outright" at President John F. Kennedy's inauguration; travels to Israel and Greece.

1962 Receives gold medal from U.S. Congress; travels to the Soviet Union to meet Premier Nikita Khrushchev; enters hospital for prostate cancer.

1963 Is awarded Bollingen Prize for Poetry; dies on January 29.

1969 *The Poetry of Robert Frost* is published posthumously.

1974 U.S. Postal Service issues a Frost commemorative stamp.

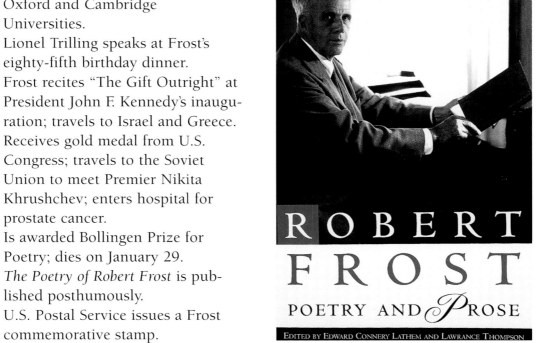

ROBERT FROST
POETRY AND *P*ROSE
EDITED BY EDWARD CONNERY LATHEM AND LAWRANCE THOMPSON

The Writer's Work

Robert Frost was primarily a lyric poet, although during his long and illustrious career he also wrote a number of dramatic and narrative poems. Along with his nine poetry volumes and the various collected editions of his poems, he wrote two famous masques, or poetic dramas, and three other minor plays, as well as essays, lectures, and letters. Frost was basically a traditional poet who used closed poetic forms, and although his poetry became increasingly philosophical and reflective, it never lost its lyrical qualities.

Although Frost's poetic career spanned the modernist period, he defined himself and his work largely in opposition to the high literary modernism of Ezra Pound and T. S. Eliot. A pastoralist by temperament and inclination, he chose to renew the vernacular tradition in American poetry. Although his poems are rich, complex, and allusive, they are also accessible to the ordinary reader. He was a self-professed "poet for all sorts and kinds," and his aim was to lodge a few poems in the popular imagination where they would not be forgotten. Frost became a literary celebrity by the end of his life, and he remains one of the preeminent American poets of the twentieth century.

Major Themes and Ideas. The complexity of Frost's poetry challenges the conventional critical notions of Frost as a pastoralist, New England regionalist, social conservative, or traditionalist—all labels which need to be qualified. Above all, Frost was a fiercely competitive, ambitious artist who viewed poetry as performance. Like the modernists, he reacted against the excesses of late Victorian melodic lyricism. Unlike the modernists, however, he did not completely reject form or rhythm for free-verse imagist poetry. He tried instead to employ the strength and fiber of vernacular speech in his work. In a series of letters to his former student, John Bartlett, Frost set forth a theory of "the sound of sense." Poetic meaning, according to Frost, derived "by breaking the sounds of sense with all of their irregularity of accent across the regular beat of meter."

Beginning with *North of Boston*, Frost tried to capture the dramatic sounds and cadences of ordinary New England speech. These sentence-sounds, or intonations, contained for Frost the essence of poetic meaning: They are apprehended by the ear, gathered from the vernacular, and captured in poetry. Frost may have used the traditional poetic forms of the lyric, ballad, sonnet, and dramatic dialogue, but he infused them with new vitality and the freshness of authentic speech. He was an expert on prosody and versification, using many subtle variations of metrical and stanzaic form. For Frost, the challenge was to renew the traditional forms, not discard them. He observed disparagingly that writing free verse was like "playing tennis with the net down."

New England Regionalist. Beginning with *North of Boston*, Frost's work took on a regional quality that led many readers to identify him with traditional, rural New England customs and attitudes. Yet Frost's relationship with his adopted region was more complex than is generally assumed. He was not a native New Englander but a San Franciscan who came to New England during his impressionable adolescent years. Even then, he did not originally live in rural New England but in the industrialized mill town of Lawrence, Massachusetts. His first forays into rural New England occurred during summer vacations, when he worked as a seasonal farmhand. Thus, he was doubly identified as an outsider. Even after the Frosts bought their farm in Derry, New Hampshire, they were slow to be accepted by locals, who disparaged Frost's farming efforts and the family annuity that helped support him.

His experience as an outsider allowed Frost to carefully observe the landscape and local culture, which eventually became the fabric of

This woodcut by J. J. Lankes of a New England rural scene was the frontispiece in the first edition of Frost's *New Hampshire: A Poem With Notes and Gracenotes.* For that work Frost was awarded his first Pulitzer Prize in 1924.

Among Frost's most memorable New England characters are Mary, Warren, and Silas in "The Death of the Hired Man"; Amy and her husband in "Home Burial"; Lafe and Dr. Magoon in "A Hundred Collars"; Loren and Mame in "Blueberries"; Sanders in "The Code"; Estelle and John in "The Housekeeper"; Maple in "Maple"; and Baptiste in "The Ax-Helve." Although some of these characters may seem curious or eccentric, Frost allows them to speak for themselves. Often they are the products of rural isolation, hardship, disappointment, or poverty. Frost does not romanticize rural life and writes from his direct recollections of teenage experiences as a summer farmhand and later stints as a poultryman, gardener, orchardist, and rural landowner.

Frost's Literary Legacy. Frost's literary influence has been widespread and significant. Virtually all modern American nature poets owe something to Frost, including such diverse poets as Robert Graves, Richard Wilbur, Theodore Roethke, William Meredith, Mary Oliver, Donald Hall, and Wendell Berry, among others. The distinguished Irish poet Seamus Heaney has generously acknowledged his debt to Frost, as has the Russian expatriate poet Joseph Brodsky. The poet and critic Randall Jarrell wrote perceptively about Frost in the early 1950s, recognizing the complexity of his work.

Since Frost's death in 1963, his standing among literary critics generally increased, with excellent studies by Richard Poirier, William Pritchard, and others. In his three-volume biography, which revealed many of Frost's character weaknesses, Frost's official biographer, Lawrance Thompson, debunked the popular stereotype of Frost as the genial Yankee cracker-barrel philosopher-poet. However,

his poetry. An artist must be an observer, and Frost's genius was to internalize the culture of rural New England so thoroughly that he came to be identified with the region. In *North of Boston,* the title of which came from real estate ads, Frost presents a remarkable gallery of rural New England character portraits.

In this collection of "New England Georgics and Eclogues," as Frost called them, one finds ordinary rural people—farmers, farm laborers, housewives—speaking from the circumstances of their lives. Frost shows great sympathy for women, the elderly, and children who struggle to express themselves or merely to be understood. Their dignity saves them from being merely grotesque.

Life was not easy for rural New Englanders in the early years of the twentieth century. Many of the characters portrayed in Frost's poems exhibit the effects of having suffered rural isolation, hardship, disappointment, and poverty. This 1901 photograph of a young New England farmer carrying two buckets with the aid of a yoke across his shoulders captures the essence of Frost's ordinary rural people.

subsequent biographies by John Walsh, Jeffrey Meyers, and Jay Parini have focused on the richness and complexity of Frost's personality. Increasingly, Frost has come to be recognized, along with Walt Whitman, as one of the greatest American poets.

BIBLIOGRAPHY

Frost, Robert. *Frost: Collected Poems, Prose, and Plays*. New York: The Library of America, 1995.

———. *The Selected Letters of Robert Frost*. Edited by Lawrance Thompson. New York: Holt, Rinehart and Winston, 1964.

———. *Selected Prose*. Edited by Hyde Cox and Edward Connery Lathem. New York: Holt, Rinehart and Winston, 1966.

Gerber, Philip L. *Robert Frost*, Rev. ed. Boston: Twayne Publishers, 1982.

Meyers, Jeffrey. *Robert Frost*. Boston: Houghton Mifflin, 1996.

Parini, Jay. *Robert Frost: A Life*. New York: Henry Holt, 1999.

Sergeant, Elizabeth S. *Robert Frost: The Trial by Existence*. New York: Holt, Rinehart and Winston, 1960.

Thompson, Lawrance. *Robert Frost: The Early Years, 1874–1915*. New York: Holt, Rinehart and Winston, 1966.

———. *Robert Frost: The Years of Triumph, 1915–1938*. New York: Holt, Rinehart and Winston, 1970.

Thompson, Lawrance, and R. H. Winnick. *Robert Frost: The Later Years, 1938–1963*. New York: Holt, Rinehart and Winston, 1976.

SOME INSPIRATIONS BEHIND FROST'S WORK

Like so many other writers, Frost was encouraged to read at an early age by his mother, a Scottish-born schoolteacher. He studied Greek and Latin poetry in high school and was thoroughly familiar with classical versification. At Dartmouth College he discovered a Victorian anthology, *Palgrave's Golden Treasury*, which introduced him to the Elizabethan, romantic, and Victorian poets. At Harvard University he fell under the influence of William James, whose works Frost studied carefully, even though he did not take a class with him.

Nature was obviously a dominant interest for Frost, and so many of his poems take their inspiration from the physical landscape of his Derry farm or from his outdoor experiences there. Frost botanized widely and enjoyed hiking and camping with his family. During his years in England, he often took long walks in the Gloucestershire countryside with his Welsh friend, the poet Edward Thomas. Their shared experiences and outlook would later be reflected in "The Road Not Taken" and other poems.

An agrarian at heart, Frost enjoyed playing the role of the poet farmer, and he always owned a farm, even though he never farmed actively. On his daily walks he was a close observer and a keen student of nature; many of his root images and metaphors are drawn from nature. Frost also enjoyed the stimulation of the academic world, though he was an unorthodox teacher. He claimed to be shy, but he was a popular public performer who went on long lecture tours each year. He was drawn to young people, especially later in life, after the loss of his wife and several of his children.

Frost had a special talent for friendship and included among his close acquaintances John Bartlett, Edward Thomas, Louis Untermeyer, Ted and Kay Morrison, and many others. During his later years, he was sought out by public figures, including President John F. Kennedy.

The apparently quiet country scene presented in Edward Hopper's 1934 watercolor *The Forked Road* (Des Moines Art Center, Des Moines, Iowa) is filled with possibilities and expectation. The artist invites the viewer to wonder what might be coming along the road or down the railroad track just beyond the edges of the painting. This interpretation of the conventional image of a fork in the road evokes the theme of Frost's poem "The Road Not Taken."

A BOY'S WILL

> **Genre:** Poetry
> **Subgenre:** Lyrics; sonnets; ballads
> **Published:** London, 1913
> **Time period:** Unspecified
> **Setting:** Unspecified natural landscapes

Themes and Issues. Robert Frost's first volume of poetry is, as the title implies, youthful in tone and outlook. Originally published as a collection of thirty-two poems with accompanying glosses, it is comprised of lyric poems that he wrote during his years in Derry, New Hampshire, before 1912. The poems are assembled in a loosely thematic sequence representing the speaker's emotional and psychological growth, from his withdrawal into himself to his return to society. Frost's wistful, late-Victorian lyrics are set within a cycle of the seasons that corresponds to his inner cycle of personal development. The volume's title alludes to an autobiographical poem by the nineteenth-century American poet Henry Wadsworth Longfellow, "A Boy's Will," whose refrain is, "A Boy's Will is the wind's will, / And the thoughts of youth are long, long thoughts."

The Poems. The poems in *A Boy's Will* are divided into three sections, which create a loose narrative sequence of the speaker's launching

Chilmark Hay by Thomas Hart Benton evokes the pastoral sonnet "Mowing," the most admired poem in Frost's *A Boy's Will.* In this painting the rhythms of scything the hay in a meadow are continued with the rhythms of loading the hay into the slowly moving horse-drawn cart.

out into the world—associated with moods of hesitation and uncertainty, which are mirrored in the seasons, weather, and natural landscape. Frost wrote to his former student John Bartlett that the book "comes pretty near being the story of five years of my life," by which he meant the early years at the Derry farm, from 1901 to 1906. However, assigning too close an autobiographical correspondence between Frost the poet and the poem's late-adolescent speaker can be misleading, as Frost's ironic glosses on the poems suggest. These glosses were later dropped from the collected editions of Frost's poems, but they provide some useful hints about his intentions. Frost also later omitted three poems from the original edition and added one, "In Hardwood Groves."

Analysis. While for the most part the poems in *A Boy's Will* do not match Frost's best achievements, some of the delicate, evocative lyrics anticipate his later work. The collection as a whole is uneven; a few major poems such as "Mowing," "A Tuft of Flowers," "Reluctance," and "My November Guest" are combined with early, less memorable poems about love and courtship. Another notable poem, "The Trial by Existence," with its evocation of the Neoplatonic myth of the preexistence of the soul, is one of Frost's most important religious poems. The most admired poem in *A Boy's Will* is the pastoral sonnet "Mowing," with its syntactical evocations of the sounds and rhythms of scything hay in a meadow.

Frost brought the manuscript for *A Boy's Will* with him when he and his family left for England in 1912, and the book was first published in London in 1913. The American expatriate poet Ezra Pound wrote a favorable review of *A Boy's Will* when it was first published and introduced Frost to English poets and writers, including the Irish poet William Butler Yeats, who praised the volume as "the best poetry written in America in a long time." The favorable reception of *A Boy's Will* encouraged Frost to collect a second volume of his verse, which became *North of Boston*.

SOURCES FOR FURTHER STUDY

Francis, Lesley Lee. *The Frost Family's Adventure in Poetry: Sheer Morning Gladness at the Brim.* Columbia: University of Missouri Press, 1994.

POETRY

1913 A Boy's Will
1914 North of Boston
1916 Mountain Interval
1923 Selected Poems
1923 New Hampshire: A Poem with Notes and Grace Notes
1928 West-Running Brook
1930 Collected Poems
1936 A Further Range
1942 A Witness Tree
1947 Steeple Bush
1949 Complete Poems
1951 How Not to Be King
1962 In the Clearing
1969 The Poetry of Robert Frost, ed. Edward Connery Lathem

NONFICTION

1963 The Letters of Robert Frost to Louis Untermeyer (with commentary by Louis Untermeyer)
1963 The Record of a Friendship, ed. Margaret Bartlett
1964 Selected Letters of Robert Frost, ed. Lawrance Thompson
1966 Selected Prose, ed. Hyde Cox and Edward C. Lathem

PLAYS

1929 A Way Out
1945 A Masque of Reason
1947 A Masque of Mercy

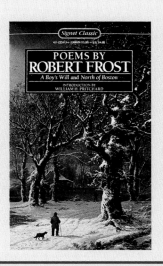

Poirier, Richard. *Robert Frost: The Work of Knowing*. New York: Oxford University Press, 1977.

Pritchard, William. *Frost: A Literary Life Reconsidered*. New York: Oxford University Press, 1984.

NORTH OF BOSTON

Genre: Poetry
Subgenre: Dramatic dialogue; monologue
Published: London, 1914
Time period: Early twentieth century
Setting: Rural northern New England

Themes and Issues. When Frost assembled the poems for *A Boy's Will* in 1913, he set aside his dramatic narratives for a subsequent volume that would become *North of Boston*. The most original and distinctive of Frost's volumes, *North of Boston* reflects his poetic theory of the "sound of sense," his belief that "the living part of a poem is the intonation entangled somehow in the syntax, idiom, and meaning of a sentence." The sixteen blank-verse dramatic narratives in *North of Boston* present incidents from the humble lives and circumstances of ordinary New England country folk. There is a strong element of local color, or regionalism, in these poetic sketches, which Frost initially conceived as a collection of "New England eclogues." Early editions of *North of Boston* noted that "'Mending Wall' takes up the theme [of the individual and society] where 'A Tuft of Flowers' in *A Boy's Will* laid it down."

Frost's original title for the collection was *Farm Servants and Other People*, indicating his interest in psychological character analysis, which was deflected from fiction to poetry. The critic Robert Langbaum notes that a dramatic dialogue must have a speaker, a listener, a conflict,

The wall in this picture is typical of the stone walls constructed as property boundary markers throughout the farmlands of New England. Stones are laid one upon the other with nothing to hold them in place except the skill of the builder. The small stones inserted into open spaces between the larger stones to achieve a tight fit often become dislodged over winter and create a shifting and weakening in the wall. The two farmers in Frost's poem "Mending Wall" are walking on either side of just such a wall, looking for open spaces that need to be shored up.

and an occasion. In employing this poetic form, Frost was much influenced by the example of the Victorian poets Robert Browning; Alfred, Lord Tennyson; and Matthew Arnold, all of whom wrote notable dramatic poetry. Frost's volume of blank-verse poetic sketches is written in a simple vernacular style more reminiscent of William Wordsworth's *Lyrical Ballads* (1798), however. Frost's character sketches contain what he variously called the "actuality of gossip" and the "abstract vitality of our speech."

The Structure. *North of Boston* originally included fifteen dramatic poems and one short introductory lyric. Frost initially included "The Pasture" as the introductory poem for *North of Boston*; it later became the introduction for his collected poems. The volume begins and ends with personal or reflective monologues, such as "Mending Wall" and "The Wood-Pile," as well as a lyric, "Good Hours." His longer dramatic dialogues, such as "The Death of the Hired Man" and "A Servant to Servants," are in the middle. There is a mixture of tone and mood in these sketches, from the comic and humorous to the pathetic and tragic. Frost employs shrewd and subtle psychological analysis of the hidden or repressed conflicts in his characters' lives, especially those of his women. These conflicts range from the death of a farmhand to the loss of a firstborn child to a desperate farmwife's inability to cope with her isolation and overwork. Throughout the volume, Frost tries to capture the distinctive New England character traits of pride, individuality, reserve, and self-reliance.

Analysis. *North of Boston* opens with one of Frost's best-known poems, "Mending Wall," a casual, discursive dialogue between two neighbors, an older and a younger farmer, who meet to walk their property lines in the annual spring ritual of repairing the stone walls that divide their property. The conversation of the two men, told from the younger farmer's point of view, becomes a study of contrasting social attitudes—progressive and traditional, open and reserved. It is not clear whether they are walling themselves in or walling each other out. The poem slyly undermines the proposition that "good fences make good neighbors." Nature, as well as the narrator, is ambivalent about walls. The central metaphor expands to become an implicit social allegory about the walls and boundaries that define self and not self, from cell walls to national borders.

"The Death of the Hired Man" retells the story of the prodigal son in Silas, the shiftless farmhand who returns to Warren and Mary in his final illness. Too proud to impose on his rich brother, Silas appears at the farm of Warren and Mary because he has nowhere else to go. The now worn-out Silas had often been an unreliable farmhand, leaving in the middle of haying season for a better wage elsewhere, as Warren recalls, but Mary is more charitable toward him. The poem's central theme turns on the meaning of home, as seen from Warren's and Mary's differing perspectives: it is either the place where people must take one in or the place where one is always welcome. The dialogue between Warren and Mary becomes a study in contrasts between traditional masculine and feminine attitudes toward mercy and justice. The poem's moral dilemma is universal, exploring the meaning of being one's brother's keeper.

"Home Burial" depicts the marital dilemma of a young couple who are trying to cope with their grief over the death of their firstborn child. The poem dramatizes the psychological differences between how men and women grieved in traditional New England culture as Amy rebukes her husband's matter-of-fact attitude toward death. The couple's conflict occurs on the stairs of their farmhouse, overlooking the family grave site. The poem in some ways reflects the Frosts' loss of their son Elliott to cholera in 1900. "After Apple-Picking" might be considered a kind of dream soliloquy, the weary poet-farmer's response to the rich abundance of his fall apple harvest, with its undertones of winter, hibernation, and sleep.

SOURCES FOR FURTHER STUDY

Kemp, John. *Robert Frost and New England: The Poet as Regionalist.* Princeton, N.J.: Princeton University Press, 1979.

Lynen, John F. *The Pastoral Art of Robert Frost.* New Haven, Conn.: Yale University Press, 1960.

Mordecai, Marcus. *The Poems of Robert Frost: An Explication.* Boston: G. K. Hall, 1991.

Walsh, John E. *Into My Own: The English Years of Robert Frost, 1912–1915.* New York: Grove Press, 1988.

THE POETRY OF ROBERT FROST

Genre: Poetry
Subgenre: Lyric poetry; dramatic poetry
Published: New York, 1969

Time period: Twentieth century
Setting: New England

Themes and Issues. After *A Boy's Will* and *North of Boston*, Frost published another eight volumes of poetry, along with his three plays and successive editions of his *Selected Poems* (1923), his *Collected Poems* (1930), and his *Complete Poems* (1949). Because his last poetry volume, *In the Clearing* (1962), was not included in the *Complete Poems*, a posthumous

The very nature of birch trees makes it easy to accept the image of a young boy using their willowy suppleness as a catapult to vault from earth to heaven. The trees in this woodcut, *Birches*, 1982–1983, by Neil Welliver, seem poised to become catapults for an adventurous youth.

volume, *The Poetry of Robert Frost*, was published to bring all of his collected work together in one volume. This volume and the later Library of America edition, *Frost: Collected Poems, Prose, and Plays* (1995), have become the definitive editions of his work.

The Poems. Beginning with his third poetry volume, *Mountain Interval*, in 1916, Frost generally included both lyric and dramatic poems, although his lyric poetry tended to become increasingly reflective or meditative in tone. Each subsequent volume contains poems of distinction, although the overall selection in each is more eclectic. The variety of poetic forms—lyric, sonnet, ballad, ode, dramatic monologue and dialogue—shows Frost's thorough command of English prosody. He never lost interest in nature or the pastoral mode, but his use of natural imagery became increasingly subtle and metaphoric.

His particular interest was in the interplay between the human and natural worlds and in the ways in which the natural world serves as an emblem or text for study. Frost's term "synecdoche," a figure of speech in which a part represents the whole, best illustrates his Emersonian concept of nature as symbol or emblem. For Frost, the natural image exists not only for itself but as the focus of human meaning. The proper understanding of metaphor becomes the essence not only of poetry but also of education. A Frost poem often expands from an initial moment of insight to what he called a temporary "clarification of life," a "momentary stay against confusion." The poem thus becomes an occasion of launching out and returning with some momentary understanding.

Analysis. Frost's sense of emblematic form helps us to understand a poem such as "Birches," with its dominant image of the farm boy swinging on birches to catapult from earth to heaven and back again. The conventional image of a fork in the road becomes a symbol of the necessity of choice in "The Road Not Taken." Frost employs synecdoche for poetic compression in such famous lyrics as "Fire and Ice," "Nothing Gold Can Stay," and "Stopping by Woods on a Snowy Evening."

Frost was one of the great modern sonnet writers, using a wide range of sonnet and sonnet-variant forms, from the Petrarchian to the Shakespearean, Miltonian, and Wordsworthian forms. Among his most famous sonnets are "Hyla Brook," "The Oven Bird," "Putting in the Seed," "Range-Finding," "Design," "For Once, Then, Something," "Acceptance," "Once by the Pacific," "Never Again Would Birds' Song Be the Same," and "The Gift Outright." His masterful "The Silken Tent" is a Shakespearean sonnet comprised of only one sentence, and "Acquainted with the Night" employs the difficult triplet rhyme scheme.

A Further Range included a number of fables or political allegories that express Frost's social conservatism and his anti–New Deal philosophy. Among his most forceful and distinctive social commentaries are "A Lone Striker" and "Two Tramps at Mud Time," with their rejection of collectivism and their Thoreauvian reliance on the individual. Other philosophical lyrics, however, such as "Desert Places" and "Provide, Provide" suggest a tacit recognition of the limitations of individualism and self-reliance.

Many of Frost's pastoral poems are also love poems celebrating courtship and married, or conjugal, love, ranging from the bitterness of "The Subverted Flower" to the gentle companionship of "West-Running Brook." He also maintained a lifelong interest in science, and many of his poems demonstrate his practical knowledge of astronomy, botany, geology, and ornithology. The range and depth of Frost's poetry challenge any easy categorization of his work and mark him as a master of richness, subtlety, and allusiveness, whose easy, colloquial style is matched by a depth and complexity of meaning.

SOURCES FOR FURTHER STUDY

Bagby, George F. *Frost and the Book of Nature*. Knoxville: University of Tennessee Press, 1993.

Brower, Reuben A. *The Poetry of Robert Frost: Constellations of Intention*. New York: Oxford University Press, 1963.

Cook, Reginald L. *The Dimensions of Robert Frost*. New York: Holt, Rinehart and Winston, 1958.

Cox, James M. *Robert Frost: A Collection of Critical Essays*. Englewood Cliffs, N.J.: Prentice-Hall, 1962.

Gerber, Philip L., ed., *Critical Essays on Robert Frost*. Boston: G. K. Hall, 1982.

Potter, James L. *Robert Frost Handbook*. University Park: Pennsylvania State University Press, 1980.

Thompson, Lawrance. *Fire and Ice: The Art and Thought of Robert Frost*. New York: Russell & Russell, 1942.

Other Works

A MASQUE OF MERCY (1947). Robert Frost's second masque is a contemporary update of the biblical Book of Jonah, set in a Greenwich Village bookstore, with a fugitive named Jonas Dove bursting in at closing time claiming to be pursued by God. Jonas believes that he has been sent to prophesy against the wickedness of the city, but he has lost faith because he "can't trust God not to be unmerciful." The other three characters, Keeper, Jesse Bel, and Paul, scoff at Jonas's convictions, claiming that God's refusal to be merciful is the beginning of wisdom. Jonas dies in the bookstore cellar, contemplating the Cross, implying that the impossibility of perfect justice throws us at the feet of divine mercy.

The small, well-stocked New York City bookstore seen in this photograph is typical of the Greenwich Village bookstore of the 1940s in which Frost set his blank-verse poetic drama *A Masque of Mercy*. The date of this photograph is unknown.

A MASQUE OF REASON (1945). During the 1940s, Frost wrote two blank-verse masques, or poetic dramas, examining the theological problems of justice and mercy. The first of these companion pieces, *A Masque of Reason*, was written as a sequel to the biblical Book of Job. It is set in a desert oasis where Job and his wife, Thyatria, are visited by God and the devil. Job questions God, once again, about why he was punished and why the wicked prosper while the good suffer. God at first evades Job's questions but then admits that he punished Job merely to show off to the devil, whom Thyatria calls God's "best inspiration." Job appeals to God for an explanation in the name of reason and human dignity but receives no satisfactory answer. The masque ends on a note of spoof, with Thyatria posing Job, God, and Satan for a photograph in front of God's throne, with no clear relationship established between merit and reward.

This desert oasis near Douz, Tunisia, shows the type of environment in which Frost placed Job and his wife, Thyatria, for their meeting with God and the devil in his blank-verse poetic drama *A Masque of Reason.*

Resources

Major collections of Frost manuscripts can be found at the University of Virginia, Amherst College, Dartmouth College, Harvard University, Yale University, the Huntington Library in San Marino, California, and the Jones Library in Amherst, Massachusetts. Other sources of interest to students of Robert Frost include the following:

Amherst Common: Robert Frost on the Web. A Web site maintained by the town of Amherst, Massachusetts; it contains information about the poet and his life. (http://www.amherstcommon.com/walking_tour/frost.html)

Frost in Cyberspace. A Web site maintained at Stephen F. Austin State University to introduce Frost to a new generation of readers, it contains biographical and bibliographic information. (http://www.libarts.sfasu.edu/Frost.html)

The Frost Farm. The site of Frost's Derry farm, outside of Derry, New Hampshire, was restored as an historic site by the United States Division of Parks and Recreation in 1976. A guided tour, interpretive film, and exhibit are open to the public. (http://www.derry.nh.us/frost.html)

The Frost Place. The farm that Frost purchased in Franconia, New Hampshire, in 1915 is now maintained by the town of Franconia as a visitor's center and summer residence for guest poets. A slide show and exhibit are open to the public.

ANDREW J. ANGYAL

Index

Page numbers in **boldface** type indicate article titles. Page numbers in *italic* type indicate illustrations.